A Beginner's Guide to Mobile Marketing

A Beginner's Guide to Mobile Marketing

Molly Garris and Karen Mishra

BUSINESS EXPERT PRESS

First published in 2015 by
Business Expert Press, LLC
222 East 46th Street, New York, NY 10017
www.businessexpertpress.com

ISBN-13: 978-1-60649-840-8 (paperback)
ISBN-13: 978-1-60649-841-5 (e-book)

Business Expert Press Digital and Social Media Marketing and Advertising Collection

Collection ISSN: 2333-8822 (print)
Collection ISSN: 2333-8830 (electronic)

Cover and interior design by Exeter Premedia Services Private Ltd., Chennai, India

First edition: 2015

10 9 8 7 6 5 4 3 2 1

Printed in the United States of America.

Karen, thank you for sharing this amazing opportunity with me. Your experience as an author and patience as a partner were so very appreciated.

Family and friends, thank you for your endless energy and support. Working alongside your successes, struggles, start ups, job hops, weddings, births, and dissertations helped inspire and push me throughout this project. Much love.

—Molly Garris

Thanks to my friend and co-author, Molly, for teaching me so much, and for making our work together so much fun!
Thanks to my family, too, for your patience as I spent all of my "free time" on this project!

—Karen Mishra

Abstract

This book is for marketers (from newbies to CMO level) who want to learn why and how to use mobile marketing to engage and convert consumers. Whether you work with a brand, retail storefront or are studying to do just that, we wrote A Beginner's Guide to Mobile Marketing to help you learn about the exploding opportunities that mobile marketing offers and why it is so important to embrace it in your integrated marketing strategy.

As you are well aware, cell phones are no longer just for calling people. Based on the latest trends in consumer behavior on mobiles, we introduce ways that marketers can use Smartphone popularity to reach people with tactics like mobile apps, mobile web, social media, search, text messaging (SMS/MMS/RMM), mobile advertising, location-based services, retail programs and more. NFC, QR codes and texting are a few pull tactics introduced, alongside push tactics like beacons, ads and in-app push notifications. Tablets require a different strategy but this book touches on that to offer background on mobile vs. tablet marketing.

Citing the latest and greatest third-party research, learn from an expert about mobile marketing, starting with the basics and ending with a roadmap to develop and measure strategic mobile marketing campaigns. Along the way, participate in exercises to ensure that you understand the material and how to apply it to the real world. Whether you are an educator, student, professional, or mobile maven, we hope that you enjoy the content and case studies we bring to life in this book.

Keywords

analytics, apps, banners, beacons, brand, case studies, display, iBeacon, integrated strategy, location-based services, MMS, mobile ads, mobile advertising, mobile at retail, mobile marketing, mobile search, mobile site, mobile web, mobile website, multi-media messaging, NFC, non-profit, omni-channel experience, push notifications, QR code, retailer, RMM, ROI, search, SMS, social, SOLOMO, sports marketing, success measurement, tablets, text messaging

Contents

Preface

This book is for marketing experts (and newbies) who want to learn why and how to create mobile marketing campaigns. With our passion for education, we wrote this to help you learn about the exploding field of mobile marketing and why it is so important to embrace it in your integrated marketing strategy. Whether you are an educator, student, professional or mobile maven, we hope that you enjoy the strategies and case studies we bring to life in this book.

Acknowledgments

Special thanks to Dr. Dale Wilson, Chair of the Marketing Department at the Broad School of Business at Michigan State University for introducing us when Molly came to MSU to present a case on mobile marketing. That was the beginning of a beautiful friendship and collaboration between an MSU Spartan and a U-M Wolverine!

Thanks, also to our expert editor, Dr. Victoria Crittenden, who is Professor of Marketing and Chair of the Marketing Division at Babson College. We are grateful for her interest in this topic and her support.

Also, a special thanks to our expert reviewers who made this book even better!

- Ian Beacraft, Manager, New and Emerging Technologies, Leo Burnett
- Chris Bridgland, Digital Strategy Director, Leo Burnett
- April Carlisle, SVP Global Shopper Marketing at Arc Worldwide
- Elizabeth Elliott, Associate Director at Starcom MediaVest Group
- Nick Fotis, Digital Strategy Director, Arc Worldwide
- Dr. Chang Dae Ham, University of Illinois, Associate Professor of Advertising
- Dr. J. Steven Kelly, DePaul University, Associate Professor of Marketing
- Chris Kenallakes, Account Director, Kenshoo
- Cezar Kolodziej, President, CEO and co-founder of Iris Mobile
- Joy Liuzzo, Principal, Product Marketing (Connected Devices) at Amazon
- Maggie Mishra, who provided us with a keen undergrad perspective

- Kurt Selden, Meredith College MBA alum and expert video game developer
- Jim Tobin, President of Ignite Social Media and author of "Social Media is a Cocktail Party" and "Earn it. Don't buy it"
- Dr. Kevin Wise, University of Illinois, Associate Professor of Advertising
- Roy Wollen, President, HANSA Marketing and Adjunct Professor at DePaul University
- Zachary Zaban, Social Media Manager at Starcom MediaVest Group

Introduction

Molly

I started working in mobile before people really understood what that meant. Their perspective on the industry was related to carriers and handset manufacturers. But third-party services didn't seem to gain traction until *American Idol* allowed us to text to vote on our favorite contestants.

I also worked in the entertainment industry with a team that created digital tools for radio stations across the United States and Canada. Knowing that text messaging was growing rapidly, we created a service, which allowed you to send text messages to radio DJs and vice versa, allowing them to send you messages about new songs, promotions, and events at the radio station. At the time, this was when an entire TXT language was beginning to take shape. Without a QWERTY keyboard or auto correction, we lived the language of LOL, L8R, BF, BFF, and more.

Even at that time, I think we knew it was a bit frustrating and craved a simpler keyboard and language but the new benefits were just too good to be true. Suddenly, I didn't have to call someone to say that I was running 10 minutes late. I could take my time deciding where to suggest we have dinner. I could even avoid a long conversation with my parents and just do a quick check in.

This service that the carriers and handset manufacturers partnered to bring us was so relevant that people began subscribing by the millions. Talking and texting was bound by bundles, far from being unlimited, which is the way it's commonly offered to us today. Except for entertainment brands though, most brands hadn't begun leveraging text messaging as a marketing tactic. I don't think it was cost prohibitive or under adopted, I just don't think brands were in the mindset of using mobile phones as marketing tools.

Today, often driven by the *always on* nature of digital devices, consumers expect informed content and services from brands. Whether it's seasonal recipes from Whole Foods or an easier way to track your workouts from Nike, people trust brands to provide these tools to enrich their lives… or at least offer a bit of entertainment. And although content and tools can often seem limitless, mobile devices and their smaller screens have forced brands to prioritize which interactions are most valuable to consumers. Creating mobile engagements is a lot like writing on a Post-It note using a Sharpie—only the most important stuff can fit.

This prioritization exercise has been useful to other communication platforms as well, ensuring we trim the fat and design around the meat, so to speak. Now brands offer focused, valuable content on mobile first; certainly the platform has influenced how brands engage people on their most personal device.

Karen

I have been teaching marketing in business schools for over 20 years, and have been fascinated by the many ways brands attempt to communicate with consumers in order to persuade them to buy. When I first read Schultz, Tannenbaum, and Lauterborn's *Integrated Marketing Communications* (1993),[1] I realized that *this* was the future of customer communication. We could not rely on just one channel to send messages to consumers, but advertising, public relations (PR), sales, and direct marketing would all have to work together to integrate our messages. We would need to better understand all of the different ways that consumers get their information throughout the day so as to help them absorb and retain the messages they get in order to make the best purchase decisions for them.

Communication decisions seemed so simple before: advertising or PR? TV or radio? Internet or mail? Now that mobile is here and connected to consumers 24/7, it is even more critical to understand all of the different ways consumers use this *new media* to get information, share brand information and reviews, talk about their favorite products, show their favorite products, and make purchase decisions. We marketers must understand *how* to leverage this new media to make sure we are helping our customers make the best purchase decision possible with the best information possible when it is most convenient for them. If we don't, our competitors will.

CHAPTER 1

Past, Present, and Future Opportunities for Mobile Marketing

For years, the running joke for *mobile marketing* practitioners was that every year a company or an influencer would name that year as *the Year of Mobile*. The year 2005 was the Year of Mobile, although in retrospect, it was the year American mobile penetration went through the roof. The year 2006 was the Year of Mobile, or more like the year that mobile data was more commonly consumed by the casual mobile phone user. Although there are certainly key milestones, it is undeniable that the last decade or so has seen immense change and development in the mobile space every single year, often even monthly.

The four key reasons for the growth and adoption of mobile include the following: (1) smarter devices, (2) smarter software, (3) faster connections, and (4) approachable pricing models. When these components align, we will see even more growth. This means that mobile marketers must be prepared with mobile strategies for those customers. See Figure 1.1 for growth in smartphone adoption.

Phone Envy

According to the Mobile Marketing Association, 48 percent of Americans never turn off their phones, and 64 percent sleep with their mobile device at their bedside.[1] Sound familiar? Could this have all started when we saw Paris Hilton and her custom jeweled SIDEKICK on the red carpet. Or President Obama exchanging e-mails on his Blackberry?

Over the years, cell phones may have changed form factors, keyboards, colors, antennas, but we always remember our first phone. One

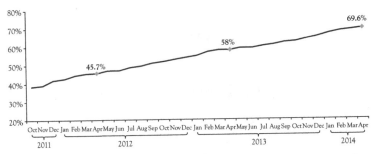

Figure 1.1 Rise of U.S. smartphone subscribers: October 2011–April 2014 (all dates reflect three-month average ending that month)

Source: Retrieved from marketingcharts.com[2]

of the most important advancements though was the introduction of touchscreen inputs. Technically, the Nokia Prada was the first touchscreen phone but the launch of the iPhone, in 2007, is what truly turned heads. Not only was the screen larger in size and sharper in resolution, its responsiveness to capacitive touch was simply a showstopper. This game-changing advancement now has today's toddlers swiping television screens and tapping on laptops. Phone envy of computer hardware manufacturers has even lead to touchscreen PCs.

We are growing accustomed to using our phones for many uses, including using them as phones, alarms, gaming systems, and even movie screens. The next evolution will allow us to use our phones to *interact with the rest of the world.* Some phones, such as the Samsung Galaxy S4, can already sniff pressure, temperature, and humidity from our environment. Their latest phone, the Galaxy S5, also packs in a heart rate monitor. Although *smartphone* technology is reaching its limits, the next advances will come in how our phones interact with the world and other devices around us.[3] That could mean using our smartphone to control our television, unlock our front door, or disarm our security system. And although most of these features are already in place, we will see more automation occurring because many of these activities can be triggered based on behavioral data. Speaking of data, big data has gotten even bigger thanks to mobile. Data are constantly transmitting from our (hand-held and wearable) devices, collecting insights about what we are doing, where we are at and who we are with, among other data points. This presents huge opportunities for marketers to organize these outputs into usable services.

OS Wars and App Stores

While Blackberry, Samsung, and Motorola were releasing more fashion-ably designed handsets, other companies focused on building *operating systems* (OS), which would soon power phones in unheard of ways. Most *feature phones*, the ones that allowed you to talk, text, and sometimes browse, were leveraging the Symbian operating system, which did not offer much customization. Consumers were reliant on the apps that came preloaded on their phone, often at the carrier's discretion.

However, when iOS, Apple's operating system was first released, this was revolutionary in the sense that the software could be opened to the development community to customize it and release what we now know as apps. Developers could download the iOS software development kit (SDK) and build apps that would reside on the phone, providing the ability to use features and functions of the phone to make a smooth, streamlined user experience. For example, the DoodleJump app leverages the phone's accelerometer, allowing a player to tilt the phone from left to right in order to navigate—no buttons or touching required.

Top smartphone platforms three-month average ending in April 2014 versus three-month average ending in January 2014 (total U.S. smartphone subscribers aged over 13)	Share (%) of Smartphone Subscribers		
	Jan-14	Apr-14	Point Change
Total Smartphone Subscribers	100.0%	100.0%	N/A
Android	51.7%	52.5%	0.8
Apple	41.6%	41.4%	−0.2
BlackBerry	3.1%	2.5%	−0.6
Microsoft	3.2%	3.3%	0.1
Symbian	0.2%	0.2%	0.0

Figure 1.2 Top smartphone platforms

Source: Retrieved from comScore[4]

With the iOS release, consumers were no longer just caught up with the latest handset but they also wanted the latest apps. Apple's iOS was the first to offer downloadable apps but by no means is it the market leader today. Overall, U.S. smartphone penetration is just under 70 percent, according to comScore. Of that, 52.5 percent use Google Android's operating system, 41.4 percent use Apple's iOS, with Blackberry, Microsoft, and Symbian sharing the small remainder.[5]

Apple's iOS came out front early, and crafted to work exclusively with Apple hardware—iPhones, iPods, and later, iPads. Additionally, iOS was launched by only one mobile carrier in the United States, Cingular, which is now AT&T. This collaboration earned Cingular exclusive rights to market the phone, earning them lots of new subscribers. The high price tag was not easy for consumers. Not only was the iPhone expensive but also this was many people's first monthly data plan to budget for. Apple fans, gadget lovers, and higher income households found themselves in an exclusive circle.

Google's Android operating system, on the other hand, was released across many handset manufacturers and multiple carriers, opening up smartphone ownership for a larger population that may not want to switch carriers or adopt costly Apple devices. It did not happen overnight but once developers saw a value in publishing apps to both the iTunes and Android Marketplace, Blackberry and feature phone owners began to get their Angry Birds on with new touchscreen devices.

Today, iOS users and iPhone sales continue to grow steadily, while Blackberry users and sales have experienced the most decline after they failed to innovate beyond being a corporate e-mail device. More financially accessible Android holds the majority stake and is known to be more of an open platform, allowing any developer to release an app on Android Marketplace, without the approval process required from Apple. Many developers and gamers prefer the control and openness that the Android platform has offered and continue to show affinity to devices using the OS.

2G or Wi-Fi?

Early Internet connections from mobile phones simply crawled. Carriers raced to build the infrastructure required to stream video and download document on these small, trending screens. 2G was upgraded to 3G, and later to 4G. Or is it? Consumers have such demand for 4G that many networks are marketing their LTE technology (which is not quite 4G speed) to their impatient audiences as 4G.

Call it what you want but phone addicts want the quickest connection possible and are willing to pay for it. According to Kirk Parsons, senior director of wireless services at J.D. Power, there is a financial impact in providing a high-performing network, as spending increases by an average of $17 per customer among those who have switched from a previous carrier to obtain a better network coverage, compared with those who switch for other reasons.[6]

Trained by connecting laptops to Wi-Fi, smartphone owners quickly realized that the fastest data connection (and cheapest!) is using a phone's Wi-Fi capability. Strong enough to power a laptop, connecting to a Wi-Fi network is just like plugging a high-speed Internet connection into your phone. And for those who do not have an unlimited data plan, the ease of browsing, sharing, and playing without the fear of cost, is a huge enabler.

Unlimited Everything

Speaking of unlimited data plans, carriers continue to carry the economic burden of building out *mobile data infrastructure*. To fund these ever-expanding networks, customers have experienced various business models to balance innovation at the lowest possible costs.

In the United States, most smartphone owners are postpay subscribers, paying a monthly bill based on a predetermined amount of data bytes. Another pricing option is buying data upfront, or prepaid. This is attractive to people with low credit scores, such as students, and help prevent costly overages. To accommodate families, shared data plans have been introduced, allowing a group of people, or a family, to share one large data package. And in emerging countries, we even see ad-supported models, which require a person to view advertisements periodically in exchange for data usage.

Regardless of what pricing model a mobile data subscriber is on, typically, once they begin using mobile data, it is quite difficult to turn back. Going online any time is often known as *data snacking*—or grabbing quick bites of information whenever or wherever time permits. To accommodate this behavior, almost all mobile carriers offer unlimited data plans, which allow a consumer the ability to use as much mobile data as they would like. This is often at a high cost, given the phone's ability to process large amounts to data required for video streaming, audio streaming, or even data streaming to other devices through a tethering feature.

Mobile Behavior

As smartphone owners now begin to demand more from handset manufacturers and carriers, they are also beginning to demand more from brands and retailers. Forrester calls this demand *the mobile mind shift* and describes it as expecting any desired information or service to be available, on any appropriate device, in context, at their moment of need.[7]

To answer this shift, marketers have been racing to build and deploy a mobile strategy that will answer consumer needs. However, what many marketers find is that when it comes to looking at behavior, nothing has really changed, aside for the immediacy aspect.

When it comes to grocery shopping, for example, people still plan their trip by looking at the circular, creating a shopping list, and clipping coupons. They just expect to be able to do these things offline, online, or on their mobile phones. Grocers such as Kroger have empowered shoppers to do these activities on their smartphones, providing convenience to those who prefer having a digital version of these tools with them in-store.

Another example might be taking a road trip. Mapping the journey, preparing music playlists, and seeking out lodging can all happen without a smartphone. However, by planning a road trip with a smartphone, a person likely completes the same behaviors but has more freedom to make changes during the trip, especially given the smartphone's ability to use a person's GPS coordinates.

Following in mobile's footsteps, we cannot forget about tablets. Results from a January 2014 survey conducted by the Pew Research Center's Internet & American Life Project, half of American adults now own a tablet or e-reader.[8] Even bigger, according to a new report from ExactTarget reveals that 73 percent of smartphone owners surveyed also own a tablet. The report also shows that tablet owners rate their number

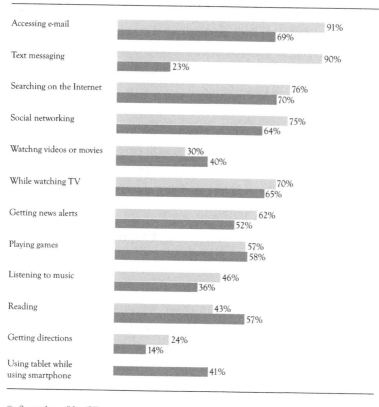

Figure 1.3 Activities performed at least once each day: smartphone versus tablet

Source: Retrieved from ExactTarget.com

one activity as searching on the Internet, versus smartphone owners who prefer accessing e-mail. Here is a comparison of tablet versus smartphone activities.[9] See Figure 1.3.

Ultimately, understanding human behavior is a key component to building a brand or retailer's mobile and tablet strategy. The most successful strategies are grounded in human truth and work to answer needs and wants. In the past, it felt like these needs were primarily surfacing *on the go* mobile use, doing things such as looking up a store's hours, getting directions, or referring back to an e-mail. Today, mobile is no longer just about mobility. In fact, 68 percent of consumers' smartphone use happens at home. And users' most common activity is not shopping or socializing but engaging in what researchers at BBDO and AOL call *me time*.[10] Whether used in or outside of the home, mobile is an indispensible tool that marketers can no longer ignore.

Many marketers feel that their tablet strategy should mimic their mobile strategy, based on similar activities that people do on the devices. While there are many parallels, most tablets stay at home or at the office, making it difficult to reach people already on the move. For marketers looking to reach people at any time and place, mobile is the strategy to set first.

The Mobile Marketing Opportunity

Initially, marketers hesitated to deliver smartphone-relevant mobile tactics such as mobile search, display, sites, and apps, fearing they would leave out feature phone users. With only text messaging and basic web browsing available for brands and retailers to reach feature phone users, they began experimenting with smartphone user-targeted tactics.

And while smartphone technology continued to improve, feature phone technology has remained relatively unchanged. Between the limited device capabilities and lack of data plan, feature phone users are just not engaging enough to make the case for marketers to accommodate them. The Yankee Group reports that smartphone owners typically surf the mobile web for 27 minutes a day, while their feature phone counterparts go online for only one minute a day.[11]

People are less and less likely to see an advertiser's television spot but with the increase in smartphone usage, they are becoming more likely to discover or seek out your brand on their phone. Channels such as the USA Network are encouraging smartphone users to join in the conversation during their program, *on the second screen.** According to eMarketer, American adults will spend an average of two hours and 21 minutes per day on devices such as smartphones and tablets doing something other than talking. That is longer than they will spend online using desktop and laptop computers.[12]

---

* http://www.usanetwork.com/social/trending

Whether an advertisement is served within a Facebook Newsfeed or in between turns on the Words with Friends app, *mobile advertisements* are a way to reach people at the right place and at the right time. These engagements are meant to drive you to learn more on a mobile website or app and hopefully drive purchase. It is estimated that mobile retail sales will reach $27 billion by 2016, up from $12 billion in 2013. Yet, only 13 percent of mobile consumers today make purchases on their mobile phones, primarily because mobile sites are not optimized properly. Instead, consumers use their phones to research products prior to an in-store purchase.[13]

It does not matter if a marketer has a thriving mobile marketing strategy in place or is just getting started, media budgets must shift from testing to employing. This is daunting to marketers. The mobile channel is new and quite different from other messaging mediums. Mobile is very much about immediacy, two-way conversation, and rich data. Marketers must build a foundation to accommodate this and navigate a fast-moving, disparate ecosystem. Not only does this require a cost investment but often challenges an organization's data and people structure.

By educating you on the various mobile tactics, how to measure its success and how to build a mobile strategy, we hope to empower you to prioritize mobile and use it to effectively reach today's consumers.

For the sake of applying these mobile tactics, pick a brand—large or small— to think about during the end-of-chapter exercises. It could be an airline, a fashion brand, a restaurant, gym, or university—anything really. By keeping this brand in mind while you read the book, you can compare what you are learning to what this brand may or may not be doing on mobile.

Exercise to Learn Concepts

Take out your smartphone and answer the following questions. Compare your results with industry averages.

Questions	Answer	Compare to industry answers
1. How many minutes per day do you use your mobile phone?		141[14]
2. What are the top activities or behaviors you do on your phone?		1. Access e-mail 2. Text message 3. Search the Internet 4. Social network 5. Use it while watching TV 6. Get news alerts 7. Play games 8. Listen to music 9. Read 10. Watch videos or movies 11. Get directions[15]
3. Did you do these behaviors before having a smartphone?		
4. What type of data plan do you have?		
5. What has changed since you got a smartphone?		
6. What brands do you interact with on mobile?		
7. Which social network do you use the most on your phone?		1. Instagram 2. Pinterest 3. Twitter 4. Facebook 5. Tumblr 6. LinkedIn[16]
8. Where are the top five places you use your smartphone?		1. In stores[17] 2. Outdoors 3. Cars 4. While traveling 5. Living room

CHAPTER 2

Calling and Messaging

Bidding Farewell to Landlines and Phone Calls

According to trade group U.S. Telecom, the number of U.S. phone lines peaked at 186 million in 2000. Since then, more than 100 million *copper lines* have already been disconnected.[1] The lines are being replaced by cellphones and Internet-based phone services. In the first half of 2013, the Center for Disease Control (CDC) found that approximately 38 percent of all adults (approx. 90 million adults) lived in households with only wireless telephones.[2] By 2016, the number of wireless-only households could climb to 50.8 million, or 42.8 percent of all U.S. residents with telephone service. Now that mobile phones are supplementing or replacing landlines, we are seeing more and more consumer-friendly tools that embrace the shift.

This shift has had a major impact on telemarketers. Recognizing that some cell phone owners are charged by the minute for incoming and outgoing calls, the FTC's Telephone Consumer Protection Act (TCPA) regulations were amended in October 2013.[3] Telemarketers will continue to be required to obtain written consent for prerecorded/auto-dialed telemarketing calls to mobile phones. Now, even informational and nontelemarketing calls made to cell phones will require prior verbal or written consent. If that is not enough, consumers can also register their phone numbers on the National Do Not Call (DNC) Registry.

In addition to telemarketing, other companies have needed to adjust to the new cell-phone only customers, as well. For example, for companies that use *Interactive Voice Response (IVR) systems*, have worked to make the systems easier for cell phone users to navigate. American Airlines offers a *Remember Me* feature that allows flyers to store up to three of their phone numbers with them. When customers call, the airline recognizes them and provides immediate access to gate and flight information, schedule changes, or cancellations. Although the feature is not limited to calls coming from mobile phones, it will certainly be useful to a traveler seeking quick information while en route to or at an airport.

Another reason that people are ditching their landline may be the new ease in *video teleconferencing* on mobile. Smartphone cameras allow callers to exchange video feeds in real-time for a crisp, clear conversation. As a result, the number of adults making video calls has tripled over the last three years, rising from 7 to 21 percent.[4] Some smartphone owners make video calls from *native phone functionality*, such as Apple's FaceTime or Android's Hangouts, and others use a variety of free apps to dial their friends and loved ones, including Skype, Tango, and more.

Video calls are not limited to personal communications. Some businesses, for example, MySkinPrescription.com, the brainchild of Dallas-based celebrity esthetician Renee Rouleau, are embracing video calls too. Renee Rouleau's estheticians are available to provide personalized skin-care coaching to women around the world through Skype and Facetime video calls. As you can see in Figure 2.1, they counsel them

Need expert advice? Get personalized skin coaching from an esthetician with a six-step consultation to help you learn about your unique skin type.

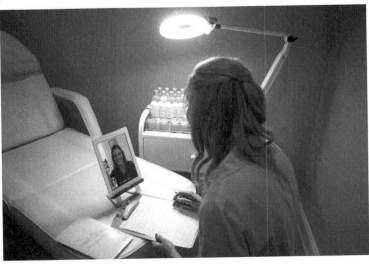

Figure 2.1 Virtual consultations
Source: MySkinPrescription.com

on everything from sun protection to nutrition to proper cleansing. We suspect more businesses will begin communicating with their customers over video calls in the future.

Hello Messaging

As one is well aware, voice calling has decreased significantly with the onset of text messaging and social media communications. When it comes to text messaging, according to the Pew Research Institute, Americans in the age group of 18 to 29 send and receive an average of nearly 88 text messages per day, and only 17 phone calls. These numbers change as people get older, with the overall frequency of all communication declining, but even in the 65 years and older group, daily texting still edges calling 4.7 messages per day to 3.8 calls per day.[5]

Short messaging system, or SMS, is a term that can be used interchangeably with text messaging, and is still the only technology used by a large majority of mobile phone owners. Eighty-one percent of U.S. adults who own a mobile phone send or receive text messages, reveals Pew Internet Research.[6] Ubiquity is only one of the many reasons why many people prefer to text instead of make voice calls. Other reasons can include ease of use, privacy, courtesy, accessibility, and time saving.

Not only do people like texting with one another but a recent study from Millward Brown Digital reveals that consumers worldwide welcome engagement with companies via mobile messaging—both to receive information from brands and to talk to brands themselves. They are even willing to provide personal data, including location, to get relevant offers. Moreover, the majority prefer SMS over other marketing channels, including video advertising, banners, and e-mail.[7]

Mobile messaging can be used to deliver coupons, facilitate promotions, drive traffic to stores, and more, but it is most commonly leveraged to deliver useful time-sensitive messages. For example, restaurants such as Firebirds are sending diners a text message when their table is ready. Pharmacies such as Walgreens are texting customers when their prescription has been refilled and is ready for pick up.

A strong *call to action* is imperative for communicating to customers why they should *opt in* to receive your text alerts and how. You may see calls to action such as:

Want to be the first to hear about our sales? Text JOIN to 12345 to get a text before we let the public in on it!

Text TACO to 23446 to get weekly news and deals from the Fiery Taco Truck

Text CONE to 34567 for a chance to win free ice cream for a year! In addition to our sweepstakes, you will also receive ongoing deals from Tasty Freeze just for signing up.

In these fictitious examples, the brands are clear about how and why to join. Typically offering something exclusive (deals, sweepstakes, or insider info) provides the best conversion.

The magic of SMS, though, is high *open rates*—some over 99 percent! Not only are the messages read, but they are read *immediately*. According to SinglePoint, 90 percent of all texts are read in fewer than three minutes from the time they are sent.*

That does not mean marketers should send text messages the way they might send e-mail. Marketers should be mindful that text messages:

- Can cost some mobile users money, especially those without an unlimited texting plan. If the message is not urgent or critical, less is more!
- Are disruptive—they display on a person's home screen, can make a sound and interrupt other mobile experiences. Be mindful of the day, time, and frequency of your message.
- Contain just 160 characters, which often becomes approximately 140 characters once legal disclaimers are added. Keep messages brief and offer a short URL to link to additional information.
- Are on a very personal device. Guidelines are in place to protect consumers from receiving spam and require marketers to obtain written consent prior to sending ongoing text alerts to consumers.

More information and guidelines can be found on the Mobile Marketing Association's (MMA's) website: www.mmaglobal.com.

---

* http://www.mobilestorm.com/

Despite the overwhelming majority of consumers who frequently use SMS, ExactTarget's research found that 49 percent of marketers do not plan to implement SMS in 2014.[8] This number continues to decrease, especially because those marketers who have employed text messaging programs are seeing great success.

Case Study: Pete's Ace Hardware Store

Pete's Ace Hardware in Castro Valley, California, has enjoyed a loyal following since 1926. However, owners Linda, Jeff, and Jason Roark wanted to drive new and repeat foot traffic, increase cart size, and increase store revenue and profit. It was also important to them for the store to stand out from local competition. The Roarks wanted Pete's Ace Hardware to continue to appeal to their existing customers, but also wanted to engage their customers through mobile offers, thereby attracting a younger, mobile demographic. So Pete's Ace Hardware began working with FunMobility to develop, launch, and track their mobile coupon campaign.

To create awareness, Pete's told customers about the Mobile Club using in-store signage, mobile search and display ads, social media advertising, and a customer base e-mail promotion. Customers could access the mobile coupons through any of the channels and via mobile, they could text PETES to 55155. Customers could use the single offer or choose to opt-in for Pete's Ace Hardware Mobile Club, enabling Pete's Ace to re-engage users with periodic coupons to their mobile phone.

Ace indicated that the program was a huge success, increasing average customer cart size by 411 percent. "49 percent of consumers who requested a coupon redeemed it, and the campaign resulted in more than 190 new customers signing up for the retailer's mobile coupon club," says Pete's owner Linda Roark. "The way that the younger generations are finding out about where to shop and other information about products is through their mobile devices, their computers, their tablets," Roark says. "Customers come into the store armed with more information than ever before, so mobile couponing is just a natural extension of them getting knowledge—they can now also get savings."

Source: internetretailer.com[9]

In addition to sending coupons, marketers can send text messages based on a customer's geography. These alerts, called *geo-fenced text alerts*, are based on cell phone tower and GPS data for people who have opted its mobile messaging program. Your local mall might send you the latest deal as you enter the parking lot or an airline may send you a status alert as you come within the proximity of the airport. These messages cost a bit more for marketers but can be highly effective.

Another type of text message marketers can opt to use is called *premium text messaging*, which allows customers to pay for something or donate toward a cause. In early days of the popular TV show *American Idol*, viewers were charged $0.99 per vote when they sent it via text message. Today, however, the more common application of premium SMS is for mobile donations. Soon after a 7.0-magnitude quake struck near capital city Port-au-Prince in January 2010, the Red Cross mobilized fundraising efforts via social networking site Twitter. @RedCross tweeted: "You can text 'HAITI' to 90999 to donate $10 to Red Cross relief efforts in #haiti." In just four days, donations via text message raised $7 million for the American Red Cross's Haiti relief efforts.[10]

Visual Messaging Is on the Rise

For marketers that favor longer form or visual messages, *Multimedia Messaging Service*, or MMS, and *Rich Media Messaging*, or RMM, are becoming more interoperable. Person-to-person MMS volume in the United States shot up to nearly 40 percent in 2012, according to CTIA's data.[11] MMS enables consumers to send and receive *one-size-fits-all* multimedia content, including photos, recorded audio, and video. As consumers become more comfortable with using their phone's camera to record and send photos and videos, they are becoming more open to receiving such content from marketers.

Because MMS and RMM are now native on a majority of feature phones, rich imagery and videos can now be played right from the inbox. The challenge with MMS is that it uses a one-size-fits-all approach and the experience degrades for multiple device resolutions. Additionally, MMS is not supported commercially across all carriers. As a result, brands have started to embrace RMM, which is a variant built to solve the problems of MMS. With RMM, the experience can be controlled, and customized content, including images, video, and audio, can be sent to each user based on their specific device capabilities resulting in a much better consumer experience and better results for the brand

Aside from directly driving sales through the holiday season, an RMM campaign is a valuable source of data for potential customers. Once users

Figure 2.2 Express Passbook of Savings
Source: Mashable.

Strong sales over the holiday season can make or break a retailer's year. Standing out from the crowd becomes even more important in a year such as 2013, when Morgan Stanley has projected retail sales to be the weakest since 2008.

Capturing the attention of potential customers is what every marketer strives to do. For their part, customers seem equally adept at tuning out unwanted advertising. But engaging and relevant content is often welcome by discerning consumers. This is the line Express is trying to walk with its RMM campaign around the company's Passbook of Savings, an annual coupon book to encourage shoppers to return throughout the season (see Figure 2.2). This year, the retail company created a digital version of the offering that centered around RMM. The campaign supported Black Friday efforts and ran from November

12 to December 3; users opted in on a landing page and received eight messages throughout the campaign.

RMM is a format pioneered by Iris Mobile. With an RMM, campaign content is tailored to the particulars of a customer's device—think of it as a coupon with responsive design. When a customer opts in, the software communicates with the handset to determine what combination of media to send. At a minimum, there are different sizes of image and text based on the phone's size. The software will also calibrate add-ons depending on the mobile device, so links won't be sent to phones without Internet access and images will automatically resize. Because Passbook is a feature found only on iOS devices, consumers won't receive a Passbook prompt unless they are using an iPhone or iPad. Social sharing options, on the other hand, are available in almost every message.

Express promoted the Pass Book of Savings (PBOS) in stores and online, with calls to action directing customers to opt in through their phones. Although a physical book could be picked up in-store, only the mobile campaign had access to all the promotions.

"We're really focused on using that mobile component to drive traffic, in store or online," says Shalini Gupta, Iris Mobile's Director of Client Services.

Because phones are such a personal medium, more care has to be taken to get permission and really provide value to the customer, or else the consumer will opt out. Holiday deals, however, tend to be welcome by consumers. RMM can be a potent tool for brands, especially in retail, to maintain a valuable connection to their customers. "We don't buy clothes every day, but we have to maintain this relationship," says Cezar Kolodziej, president and CEO of Iris Mobile. Although consumers might not buy from a brand every day, frequent interactions over a long-term basis would mean your brand will be the first company that comes to mind when the consumer decides to make a purchase.

Although mobile messaging can be perceived as invasive and brands should tread lightly, the added Tender Loving Care (TLC) pays off—open rates are five times higher for mobile messaging than for traditional e-mail marketing, says Kolodziej, and the opt-out rates are lower than for traditional text message campaigns. Plus, because the coupon stays on the phone, there's no need to follow a link to get to the promotion at the point of sale, making redemption seamless on the customer's end.

One of the main Key Performance Indicators (KPIs) a brand analyzes for an MMS campaign is open rates, which so far have been *excellent* for the Express campaign. Social shares and click-through rates are also tracked, and the coupons include unique codes so Express knows how many offers are redeemed. Iris says 35 percent of consumers who are sent an RMM go on to make a purchase, either online or in-store, whereas average redemption rates for traditional SMS messages are 16 percent.

opt in, brands can tailor content and target its messaging to improve the campaign's efficacy. Therefore, MMS clients have access to analytics that are not available in other messaging channels, and as the Metrics That Matter series has illustrated thus far, data is money. Of course, that data needs to be combined with an understanding of consumer behavior to best market to your audience and drive return-on-investment or ROI.

"It's the innovation piece. It's not just simply sending the image. It's being smart about how we're communicating with the audience," says Gupta.

Express' Black Friday campaign was just one part of the brand's mobile efforts (see Figure 2.3), which includes an app that offers mobile payment via a digital version of the company's Express Next credit card.

Trending Now: IM Apps

Instant messaging (IM) apps, whether preinstalled on smartphones or downloaded from an app store, have also been seeing increased usage among both teens and adults. Although it is a disparate ecosystem with many different messaging apps, each provides the opportunity to avoid per message SMS and MMS costs that the carriers charge in the native messaging functionality. Instead, people chat over a data connection or using Wi-Fi.

Figure 2.3 Express' Black Friday campaign

Source: mashable.com[12]

Experian data from 2013 showed 23 percent of smartphone users accessed IM and chat apps such as Kik Messenger, WhatsApp, and Google Talk during a typical week.[13] Adoption is growing rapidly and brand marketers are beginning to take note. Aquafina FlavorSplash, for example, recently partnered with Kik to launch their first branded IM sticker pack.[14] See Figure 2.4.

On Snapchat, a visual messaging app, Taco Bell was one of the first brands to launch an account. See Figure 2.5. Followers receive snaps (an image, video, or series of video clips) that can only be viewed for 10 seconds or less, which then self-destruct after being viewed. Taco Bell used the platform to message fans about the reintroduction of the Beefy Crunch Burrito. "*People are obsessed with the Beefy Crunch Burrito so Snapchat seemed like the right platform to make the announcement*," Taco Bell director of social and digital marketing Tressie Lieberman told Mashable. "*Sharing that story on Snapchat is a fun way to connect with the fans that we are thrilled to have. It's all about treating them like personal friends and not consumers.*"[15]

Figure 2.4 Image of Aquafina FlavorSplash stickers on Kik

Source: http://cashmereagencydemo.files.wordpress.com/2013/10/screen-shot-2013-10-18-at-5-30-01-pm.png

Figure 2.5 Image of Taco Bell's SnapChat announcement on Twitter

Source: https://www.chownow.com/wp-content/uploads/2013/08/Taco-Bell-Tweet.png

Figure 2.6 Examples of Taco Bell's SnapChats[16]

The Almighty E-mail

Blackberry began powering e-mail on mobile devices for early business adopters who needed to get their messages while away from the office. Today, studies report that about half of all marketing e-mails are opened on a mobile device rather than on webmail or desktop.[17] Looking ahead, Forrester Research predicts that 78 percent of U.S. e-mail users will also access their e-mails via mobile by 2017.[18] It is no longer just about business. According to AYTM Market Research, U.S. mobile e-mail users mainly use it for personal reasons (59 percent) versus work reasons (5 percent) or both (30 percent).[19]

Marketers looking to push their message to mobile devices find e-mail to be an important linchpin to their mobile strategy. Of the total estimate for U.S. mobile marketing spent in 2013, the Mobile Marketing Association (MMA) projected that just over 41 percent (approx. $4.27 billion) was expected to be spent on mobile customer relationship management (mCRM) efforts. Looking ahead, they project mCRM to be around $7.68 billion in 2015.[20] That spending will be used for activities such as designing messages to be optimized for mobile, ensuring an optimized postclick landing page or website and conducting subject line tests that drive reads, not deletes.

There are many opportunities to cater e-mail messages to a mobile user. Catchy subject lines, smaller amount of content, and larger fonts are just a few best practices. Design is important as well. Similar to mobile website design, there are several options for mobile-friendly formatting:

1. *Mobile-friendly or mobile-aware design:* This is a one-size-fits-all strategy that simply reduces the width of messages, separates calls to action with more cushion to avoid accidental clicks on mobile.
2. *Responsive design:* This is an HTML layout that adapts for different devices and screen sizes. It allows you to rearrange or constrict content on smaller screens without designing and coding two completely different e-mails. It is most effective when applied to template e-mails.
3. *Real-time templates:* New technologies allow you to create specific messages in real-time that will appear when the e-mail is viewed on certain devices. For example, you can program a different image to

Figure 2.7 Mobile e-mail design style examples[21]

appear in the e-mail if it is opened on a desktop, and make the call-to-action simpler on a mobile device.

Studies show that marketers who adjust their e-mails to the mobile platform have boosted *click-through rates* up to 63 percent and *transaction rates* up to 18 percent.[22] To learn more about design formats best practices, look to e-mail platforms such as Litmus, MailChimp, ExactTarget, and Constant Contact for the latest and greatest. We have included a few links in Chapter 8.

Measuring Success

For marketers who offer a phone number to call, success is getting your customer the correct information as quickly and easily as possible, especially knowing they may be on the go or could potentially come into poor cell phone reception. One of the biggest failures of integrated marketing is to forget to include a phone number or a way to give the customer a way to follow up after they have seen a message. One option is to offer a customer satisfaction survey at the end of each call but a more common measurement is to look at average call lengths and work to shorten them.

Those who are testing video conferencing will probably focus on qualitative measures such as overall experience and ease of use for their customers and quantitative measures such as sales conversions from traditional calls to video calls.

Text messaging and e-mail programs are measured similarly to one another. *Churn*, or opt-out rate, is a key factor, which measures the percentage of your subscriber base that leaves your database over a certain measure of time. Marketers continuously work to lower churn by gathering data about their subscribers such as:

- Are they opening messages?
  - *This is known as an open rate. If not, was the subject line appealing? Or did we send a similar communication too recently? Getting to the correct frequency is different for every business and often every customer.*
- What days and times are they opening messages?
- Which links and types of calls to action are they clicking on to learn more?
- What products or services has this customer bought in the past? How can we target the correct content to them?

These are a few insights which help marketers better customize messaging programs over time and provide more value to their loyal subscriber base.

Leaning on the Experts

Each of these tactics requires deep *channel knowledge* to execute programs. For example, text messaging programs must be approved by carriers through a specific process and e-mail optimization is often specific for various Internet service providers and e-mail clients. Small businesses might like to start with all-in-one platforms such as Trumpia,* whereas larger organizations may need channel-specific expertise from some of the case study providers mentioned earlier.

---

* http://trumpia.com/

Exercise to Learn Concepts

Sign up for at least two text messaging programs and observe the messages you receive, how frequently you receive them, how valuable the messages are and if they contain images and video or just text. Compare and contrast the programs to determine what you might do differently if you were managing the brand.

If you have not seen any signs in your favorite stores or restaurants, try the following:

- Bed Bath and Beyond—text OFFER1 to 239663
- Express—text EXPRESS to 397737
- Fandango—text your zip code to FNDGO (36346) and get a text back with movie show times near you
- Macy's—text JOIN to 62297

To *opt out* at any time, just reply STOP.

Exercise to Apply Concepts

Think back to the brand that you selected at the end of Chapter 1. What might be some ways this brand would use voice calls to better automate their business? Is there a place for video calls and consultations? How might they use SMS, MMS, or RMM? Would mobile-optimized e-mail make sense for them? What content would be used for each tactic?

CHAPTER 3

Search and Web

Every Business' Workhorse

It is critical for brands to be present and accounted for when consumers use their smartphone to search. Given the increase in people adopting smartphones and the convenience of always having our phone within arm's reach, it should not be a surprise that *mobile search* is expected to surpass desktop search by 2015.[1] Whether we are looking up a business address, hours of operation, or just getting inspiration on vacation destinations, marketers who do not appear in search results miss prospective sales leads. If a marketer appears in the results but does not deliver a mobile-friendly web experience, they not only miss a lead but potentially a conversion too.

Mobile Is Not Just about Mobility

Mobile activities, as we discussed earlier, are not limited to *on the go*. As you can see from Figure 3.1, Google and Nielsen find that the majority of searches done on mobile happen from home.[2] Mobile is as much about *convenience* as *mobility*.

Although a PC may be within reach, more and more people are reaching for their phones to search, instead. In fact, in the United States, total *searches* on the PC dropped 6 percent year-over-year.* Speed and convenience drive 81 percent of mobile searches. Whether it is the ease of remaining seated or not wanting to wait for your laptop to fire up, people are willing to search across a variety of categories from News to Food.

According to Google, people search Arts and Entertainment, News, and General Knowledge the most. However, mobile search is contextual and will vary in frequency depending on where a person is. For example,

---

* https://www.comscore.com/Products

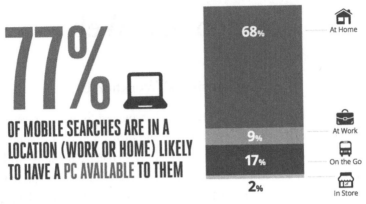

Figure 3.1 Google Nielsen statistics on where people use mobile search

people search for Restaurants most often when they are on the go or at work, versus while at home or at school.

Location, Location, Location

Search engines have replaced the Yellow Pages. To locate something nearby, we no longer need to sort through results based on each location. Rather, our smartphones help us share our GPS coordinates and offer search results based on certain proximity. Let's say I open my smartphone browser and search for *Coffee*. I won't just see links related to coffee. Rather, I will also see local coffee shops that can be filtered based on criteria such as *within half mile, within one mile, five miles*, and so forth (Figure 3.2).

This ease of search, worked and reworked to improve *clicks*, has made local search one of the most common smartphone behaviors. In fact, a new study released by Google reveals that 84 percent use search engines on their computer or tablet and even more (88 percent) do so on their smartphone. What's even more powerful is the actions taken after searching. Research shows that within a day of a local search, 34 percent of consumers who sought local information on their computer or tablet made their way to a store, and of those who used a smartphone,

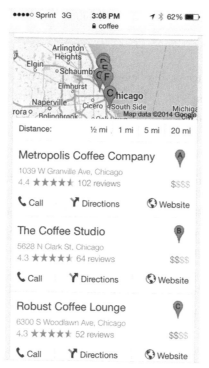

Figure 3.2 Example of a Google search engine result for coffee. The searcher was in Chicago so the results are localized

the number is even higher at 50 percent. Sales also reflect the power of local search. Eighteen percent of local searches on smartphone lead to a purchase within a day versus 7 percent of nonlocal searches.[3]

Other features that have helped accelerate mobile search conversions include one-touch calling or *Click to Call,* one-touch directions or *Click for Directions,* and one-touch website redirect or *Click for Website.* Forty-nine percent of searches for local businesses occur without a specific business in mind. These shortcuts accelerate follow-up actions and help a person dig deeper into a result.

As data becomes more accurate and more easily distributed, search results will continue to offer more contextually relevant information. From mobile search results, the *top three reasons* consumers went on to *click to call* a business were as follows:

1. Check business hours (52 percent);
2. Make a reservation or schedule an appointment (51 percent); and

3. Inquire about inventory, availability, or booking information (47 percent).

Mobile apps such as Yelp and OpenTable are beginning to offer this type of information so it is likely in the best interest of search engines, such as Google, Yahoo, and Bing, to incorporate these types of information as well, in an effort to further drive conversion for their advertisers.

Search Is an Omni-channel Effort

Recognizing the volume and importance of search across mobile and tablets, businesses that invest in search engine marketing will now see their efforts translate across platforms for an *Omni-channel experience.*[4]

> Simply put, (Omni-channel marketing) is the notion that consumers use more than one channel (web, catalog, mobile, store) to make a purchase. The idea reflects the fact that consumers don't see channels, they seek solutions: either a retailer satisfies a need or it doesn't. Increasingly, consumers use digital channels to make a purchase decision even if that purchase is ultimately completed in a store.[5]

Although there may have been a separate search investment on mobile in the past, that is no longer the case. Some marketers refer to this as integrated marketing[6] or multichannel marketing,[7] yet the term Omni-channel marketing reflects a focus on solutions, which is what will ultimately satisfy customers.

To ensure search dollars aren't wasted, marketers must now have their web experiences *optimized* across devices. If they do not, search engines will punish them by lowering their search ranking over time, just as they do with other factors such as quality score. That means, while a brand might be spending the same amount of search dollars as a competitor, and if their web destination requires a lot of zooming and pitching, or some parts not loading at all, it's more difficult for the search engine (e.g., Google, Bing) to convert the searcher to the desired action. Over time, the search engine algorithms will feature the competitor's easy-to-use site to ensure that consumers have a great experience and will take the desired action to convert.

Not only is a mobile-friendly website important for search rankings, but consumers expect it these days. A recent study by Compuware revealed that 57 percent of consumers said they would not recommend a business with a poor mobile experience, and 40 percent said they would switch to a competitor offering a better one.*

After searching for a local coffee shop in Chicago, here is how the websites of three top search results looked. Although all the three sites were functional on mobile, we thought Figure 3.4 looked most inviting with rich colors and simple navigation using three blocks to show prioritized features. Figure 3.5, though, is most user friendly. It is optimized for mobile so there is no zooming or pinching required. This prevents accidental clicks, which can frustrate a user, and simplifies the purchase process (Figures 3.3 to 3.5).

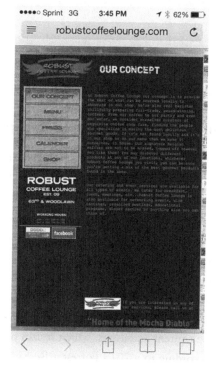

Figure 3.3 Mobile website for RobustCoffeeLounge.com

---

* http://www.compuware.com/en_us/application-performance-management.html

Figure 3.4 Mobile website for MetropolisCoffee.com

Designing a Cross-Platform Web Experience

Websites of the past may or may not load on mobile devices, mainly due to the code that mobile devices can or cannot support. For example, few phone browsers will load *Flash animation*—a common interactive web language that was very common on desktop websites. To provide a great web experience across devices, marketers mainly have two options: Build their website using responsive design or create device-specific versions of their website.

Many marketers are building or rebuilding their website using *HTML5 code* and responsive design to be sure it will be useable across mobile devices, tablets, and desktop computers. This results in a single site, with the same content and assets, which resizes based on the screen it is loaded on. According to a 2013 Forrester Research survey, approximately 45 percent of mobile marketers are using HTML5 sites.[8] Figure 3.6 depicts how content blocks shift as the devices change in size.*

---

* http://www.creativebloq.com/responsive-web-design/problems-8122790

Figure 3.5 Mobile website for IntelligentsiaCoffee.com

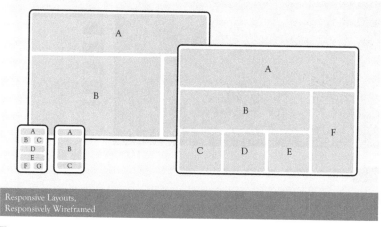

Figure 3.6 Responsive layouts, responsively wireframed by Adobe's James Mellers

Responsive design is extremely search engine friendly and designers are quickly adopting standards for this new approach. Try loading Starbucks. com on a desktop, tablet, and mobile device. This is a great example of responsive design implementation (Figures 3.7 and 3.8).

There are some downsides to responsive designing. The CSS style sheets used are not always supported by older browsers so visitors might see a small-sized design instead of a full screen view. Other challenges with responsive design include challenges with cross-platform navigation bars, image loading, and testing. The more designers experiment, the more information will help standards to form though, making these experiences easier to deploy.

If a marketer isn't ready to *re-platform* (completely re-build) their existing website, they may opt to build device-specific sites. This means that the navigation, content, and overall design can be targeted to a device.

For example, if you are a retailer, you may want to prioritize the store locator on a mobile web version of the site instead of prioritizing a weekly circular, which might not load well on mobile. Often these experiences will be served on the same domain as a desktop site but have a slightly different URL (e.g., http://m.macys.com). As soon as a consumer visits

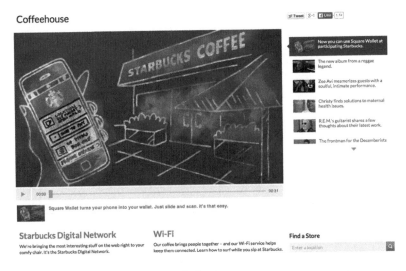

Figure 3.7 Starbucks.com on desktop

Figure 3.8 Starbucks.com on mobile

http://www.macys.com, a line of code understands that they are coming from a mobile device and quickly redirects them to the mobile-friendly version. It is quick and seamless and more often than not, the user never notices a difference.

Typically, a separate mobile website has a *stacking navigation* and more compact content that requires less scrolling. Figures 3.9 and 3.10 show two examples of a mobile-specific website: Macys.com (left) and CVS.com (right).

Device-specific sites are great for customizing the experience based on the device a consumer is on but they are more expensive and time-consuming to maintain because there are one or more versions to host, design, maintain, and test.

Regardless of the type of design you use, a mobile-optimized website is a great investment to reach the ever-expanding mobile search and browse user base.

Figure 3.9 Macys.com offers a grey buttons that compile to form a stacking navigation

Optimizing for Mobile SEO

Similar to desktop web, once you build a mobile website, your work is not finished. Rather, marketers must anticipate making ongoing updates and improvements to continuously optimize their site's findability and usability. Although there is no definitive list of optimizations to make, Google has released guidelines to help webmasters understand what changes could increase their search rankings.

Some of those tips include:

- Host your mobile website on the same domain as your desktop website, for example, if your website is www.ferrari.com, host your mobile experience on m.ferrari.com or www.ferrari.com/mobile versus www.ferrari.mobi.

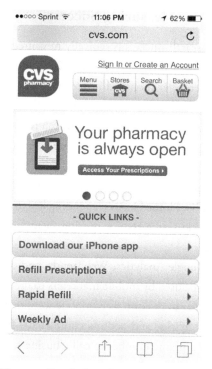

Figure 3.10 CVS.com offers light silver buttons that compile to form a stacking navigation

- Ensure your mobile site will be indexed by search engine crawlers with activities such as submitting an xml sitemap and properly linking web content to the equivalent mobile content.
- Use videos that are playable on mobile websites because some desktop sites may use Flash to play video, which is not always supported on mobile browsers.
- Improve page load times to render in less than one second on mobile.

Additional tips and resources are available on the Google Web-masters resource site: https://developers.google.com/webmasters/smartphone-sites/.

Measuring Success

Similar to desktop search, success is typically measured by *Cost per Click* (CPC)—or the cost for every time the advertisement is clicked and *Cost per Mille* (CPM)—cost per thousand impressions or times the advertisement is served. For each, the smarter and more efficient your advertising is, the more often consumers click on your search result or simply see the ad words you chose as a search result. The more efficient the ad, the lower the cost.

For example, let's say Home Depot pays a $2 CPC on search and Lowe's pays a $3 CPC. Home Depot is spending less to get mobile searchers to click on their ad search results, making them more successful than their competitors.

For websites, Google Analytics, WebTrends, and other desktop analytics tools can also be used by mobile marketers to measure and optimize their presence. Similar to desktop web, mobile website performance metrics are often visits, clicks, and actions completed—for example, filled out a form, clicked a phone number to call a business, and so forth. Also like desktop web, retailers with brick and mortar stores have difficulty tracking conversion from search to in-store conversion. Some marketers deploy search campaigns that use unique promotion codes. These not only offer shoppers a discount but when used in store, the retailer will know that these shoppers engage with their search campaign. Google is piloting more sophisticated data matching programs to track Ad Words to in-store conversions,[9] but today, understanding how digital campaigns convert in-store still remains the Holy Grail to marketers.

Different from desktop web, mobile browsers do not support cookies for tracking. Therefore, re-targeting isn't possible and certain metrics such as time spent on a mobile site cannot be determined. This may also be appealing for mobile consumers, as they will ultimately prefer mobile search over desktop search in order to maintain their search privacy.

Additional qualitative research can be done to test the *usability* of the site—or the ease at which consumers have browsing or completing an action. It is becoming more and more common for web developers to create prototypes to use for early consumer research. The quicker they can learn what consumers like and dislike, the quicker they can make changes to be user centric.

Figure 3.11 Corvette Coupe mobile site

Source: Chevrolet.com*

---

*http://m.chevrolet.com/corvette-stingray.html

Case Study: Chevrolet

Chevrolet turned toward their global mobile agency of record, Acquity Group, to help them redesign their mobile website. To align with consumer expectations and maintain their reputation as an industry leader, Acquity Group worked with Chevrolet executives and marketing team members to develop a series of immersive mobile experiences. One, for example, was for the 2014 Corvette Stingray.

To highlight the redesign of the iconic Corvette, including the re-emergence of the legendary Stingray, a mobile site experience was released during the 2013 North American International Auto Show. The site quickly attracted the attention of visitors in high volumes, effectively doubling Chevrolet's mobile traffic overnight and successfully generating consumer enthusiasm for the redesigned 2014 Corvette Stingray.*

The Corvette mobile website sits within Chevrolet.com or can be accessed through mobile search, mobile display, or directed at: http://m.chevrolet.com/corvette-stingray.html. The site allows users to swipe through a number of videos and pictures of the car and its features. As you can see in Figures 3.11 a, b, and c, users can view the car in different colors and with different wheels, as well as find nearby stores and special offers.

---

* https://www.acquitygroup.com/work/project/detail/work-general-motors

Exercise to Learn Concepts

When you use your phone to search, what are *the top five things* you search for? Here are the options: Arts and Entertainment, Auto, Beauty, Finance, Food, General Knowledge, Health Care, Home Furnishing, Navigation, News, Social, Tech, Travel, and Shopping.

Rank your top search terms	Compare to Google–Nielsen Data
1.	1. Arts and Entertainment
2.	2. News
3.	3. General Knowledge
4.	4. Shopping and Food
5.	5. Tech and Healthcare

Exercise to Apply Concepts

Think back to the brand that you selected at the end of Chapter 1. What might be some search terms that you would buy for them to ensure a consumer sees their search results? Do they have a mobile-friendly website? Describe why it is (or is not) mobile friendly. Make recommendations for improvement.

CHAPTER 4

Mobile Applications (Apps)

App Mania

In addition to using mobile websites to browse for information, 90 percent of smartphone owners download *mobile apps* to access information.[1] Of these app users, a recent Compuserve survey revealed that 85 percent prefer mobile apps to mobile websites. Users believe apps to be

- more convenient (55 percent);
- faster (48 percent); and
- easier to browse (40 percent).[2]

App icons allow for quick, easy access to a brand's or service's content, so they are especially useful for those you revisit frequently. Apart from the convenience of the icon shortcut, apps also create a superior experience by tapping into a smartphone's *features and functionalities*. Features such as the microphone, the accelerometer, and the GPS coordinates can be leveraged to create seamless actions.

For example, Gibson Guitars released the *Learn & Master* app (Figure 4.1). When the app is open, the Tuner Tool uses the phone's microphone to listen to the guitar's sound and provide the player with feedback on how to get it in tune.

Mobile websites are getting more sophisticated, now being able to pull a person's GPS coordinates, but the richest experiences can only be built within an app and the best apps take full advantage. Think about Facebook. To find friends using Facebook, the app accesses your phone's Contacts to see who else is registered on the site. To add a picture, you don't have to take it within Facebook. You can upload it from your Camera Roll/Photos history. To share your location, there is no need to type in an address. The app uses your phone's GPS to help you choose where you

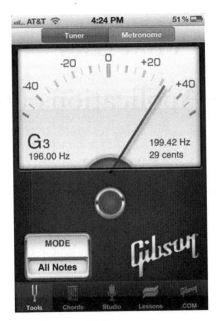

Figure 4.1 Gibson's Learn & Master App

Figure 4.2 Facebook App showing a post that includes location

are. These conveniences are what make an app great and the reason people come back time and time again. For years, big brands debated if they should build a mobile app or mobile site. It's no longer a debate—your consumers will likely demand both (Figure 4.2).

How Apps Work

Similar to downloading software such as Microsoft Word onto your computer, mobile apps are tiny software programs that will remain on a person's phone until deleted. Some apps may come *pre-installed* on your new phone either installed by the carrier (e.g., AT&T Barcode Scanner) or by the operating system (e.g., Google Maps). Most commonly, people *download apps* from their phone's operating system app store (e.g., iTunes, Google Play.)

Most *branded apps* are free to download. However, apps with advanced functionality or licensed content might require a nominal fee to download. These are called *paid apps*. Apart from free and paid apps, there is one other kind called *free-mium*. This is when an app is free to download but premium features are available for a cost, such as an ad-free feature, an extra level or tool, or *virtual good*. Among the free, paid or free-mium apps, many are ad-supported, or display advertisements to help support the cost of development.

Let's use Words with Friends Free as an example. It was free to download but offers in-game purchases such as the Word-o-Meter tool so it's considered a free-mium app. It also serves ads in between turns so it can also be described as ad-supported. For those that are bothered by the ads, Words with Friends is also offered as a paid app and for $4.99 (iOS version), the game can be played without seeing ads in between turns (Figures 4.3 to 4.5).

In September 2013, Business Week looked at the Top Grossing Apps according to AppAnnie.com. Mobile games make up nine of the 10 top-grossing apps in Apple's App Store (Pandora was the exception). Only one of those charged for a download: Infinity Blade 3, which costs $6.99.[3] This means people expect apps to be free but are becoming more comfortable with in-app purchases and the ads that support them.

App publishers can add or remove their app from an App Store at any time, such as we saw with the publisher of Flappy Bird.[4] Publishers

Figure 4.3 Words with Friends Free in-game purchases

*Figure 4.4 Words with Friends Free in-game purchases
Word-o-Meter tool*

Figure 4.5 Full screen advertisement that appeared in between turns on Words with Friends Free

can also adjust the price and are expected to make ongoing updates to ensure it works on the latest operating system releases. Although there are millions of apps in the app stores, a few lucky developers may be featured within the app stores. This special placement cannot be bought with a *media buy*—it is reserved for clever apps that cut through the clutter. This is one of the top ways that people learn about new apps so it's a very coveted spot. People also hear about apps through word-of-mouth, advertisements, or on the app stores' top lists. Top lists are generated based on the number of times this app has been downloaded over the course of one week. Although this placement also cannot be bought, app publishers can be strategic about using a high volume of advertisements in a short time span so that the app can achieve a popular listing and begin to see *organic downloads* based on that listing.

Although there are literally millions of apps available, the average smartphone owner downloads just 41.[5] Many people download an app and delete it immediately or never open it at all. They may have found it difficult to use, not what they had expected, or unnecessary to have on their phone. To prevent this from happening, developers should partner with marketers to create messaging that communicates what the app does and why people need it. Screenshots and short video clips also help.

People may not have that many apps but the ones they have, they use a lot. According to mobile analytics provider, Flurry, the U.S. consumer spends an average of two hours and 38 minutes per day on smartphones and tablets: 80 percent of that time (two hours and seven minutes) is spent inside apps.[6] To say apps have become engrained in our lives is an understatement.

In a separate survey of 2,000 consumers, checking apps was by far the most common part of their morning routine, with 80 percent of smartphone users using apps to check e-mail, weather, news, and traffic.[7] In the evening, the mobile app audience rivals the viewership of the top three TV networks during prime time, at 52 million at 8 p.m.[8] This is especially true with mobile-carrying Millennials, 32 percent of whom are using apps in the evening, providing marketers with a captive audience who may engage with them or see their ad.

Push notifications is a common tactic that app developers use to spark repeat visits to their app. For users who chose to allow notifications, only urgent and important information should be pushed. For users playing a game, it's important to know when it's your move or turn to play. For a news app, big, breaking stories may warrant a push notification whereas a smaller, local story would not. Marketers should balance how many push notifications they send (Figure 4.6). If they bombard a person, they risk the user turning off notifications or worse, deleting their app.

Owning an App

App design principles are similar, if not the same, to mobile site designs. However, a key difference between apps and sites is the development process. One mobile site *code base* can be used to reach all smartphone owners. Conversely, with mobile apps, the code base varies by operating system. For example, iOS uses Objective-C and Android apps use Java. To build apps across the different platforms, brands and services often employ platform-specific developers because most developers do not necessarily know every language or the ins and outs of the operating systems.

Figure 4.6 Push notification examples from Kraft's iFood Assistant App and Zynga's Scramble with Friends App

Thankfully, each operating system releases a software development kit (SDK), which guides developers on how to design and build apps native to their platform.

Based on the time and cost to develop an app for several platforms, some brands and services may consider deploying a *hybrid app*. This is an app that simply frames a website. A hybrid app typically does not leverage push notifications or the phone's features and functionalities. Rather, it frames the website for the users that prefer an app on their phone's screen. Feature-rich apps such as the Gibson Guitars and Facebook apps mentioned previously, could not adopt this approach. However, a blog or simple news feed or list of products, such as Banana Republic, could (Figure 4.7).

Regardless of the development approach, apps must be tested and updated whenever a new software release is pushed to phone users. For example, some Android users might be using Jelly Bean (version 4.3), whereas others may have adopted Kit Kat (version 4.4)—an app must be compatible for both. Based on this extra level of complexity, marketers need to plan for ongoing maintenance cost to keep apps up-to-date and

Figure 4.7 Banana Republic App, a hybrid app example

bug free. Users have a low tolerance for buggy apps. Recent research from Compuserve shows that 79 percent of app users would only retry an app once or twice if it failed to work the first time.[9]

Alongside the extra cost, app developers must also be mindful of Apple's App Store approval process.* All apps must be submitted to Apple for a standards review and performance test. Although developers need to add extra time for this (anywhere from a few days to a few weeks), the process ensures safety and relevancy.

Android does not implement an approval process and as a result, Trend Micro reports that there are over one million malicious apps currently available for download on the Android market.[10] This causes consumer distrust with data security. In fact, mobile phone app makers have the lowest levels of trust among consumers, ranking lower than

---

* Retrieved on May 19, 2014 from https://developer.apple.com/app-store/review/

their mobile services provider, utility company, employer, and doctor. To ensure safety, Android users can turn to security companies such as Norton and McAfee, who are creating their own apps, which scan and protect against security risks. *Mobile app makers must ensure security in order to build consumer trust.*

Measuring Success

Many app developers are consumed by acquisition or how many people have downloaded, or acquired, their app from the app stores. *Churn* is only one indication of success though, because some figures show that as many as 80 to 90 percent of apps are uninstalled after using it just once.[11] To prevent users from dumping your app, consider *tutorials* to show them how to use and make the most of your app (Figures 4.8a and b).

Another app success measure is *frequency of use*, or how many times an app user opens his or her app. High frequency might be critical for a

Figure 4.8a WebMD app welcome page

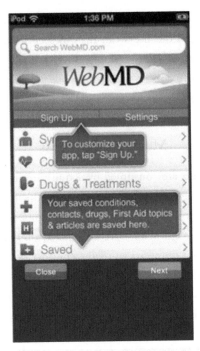

Figure 4.8b WebMD tutorial for first-time app users

news app such as CNN or music streaming app such as Pandora, which rely on ad impressions for a significant portion of revenue. However, for an insurance claims app such as Allstate, drivers do not get into car accidents very often so they may not be as concerned about a lower frequency.

Like websites, other app measurements include time spent in the app, which features are being used, and if a user is taking the desired actions—buying, clicking on ads, and so forth. To monitor these activities, app developers use tools such as Flurry to track in-app activity, whereas overall app downloads can be provided by the app stores.

Case Study: Carolina Hurricanes Mobile App—Coop Elias, Social Media Manager for the Hurricanes

The Hurricanes had a mobile optimized site, but didn't have a mobile app. They were offered the opportunity to share in the National Hockey League (NHL) league-wide mobile app initiative, which was a shell, free of charge. They decided to go with this option, knowing that the NHL would be more knowledgeable about hockey and their needs than starting with another vendor outside of hockey.

The Carolina Hurricanes Official App, available on iOS and Android, and offers fans features such as real-time shift changes, enhanced game stats, post-game video highlights, customized game alerts, player profiles, and more. Also, the integration with the league is a bonus because it provides fans with seamless communication from team to team.

To promote the app, Coop Elias made sure that app announcement was a top story on the Hurricanes website, where it encouraged fans to download the app, promising even more features and updates than they could get from the current website. Of their current users, 73 percent use the iOS version (19 percent of that 73 percent being on iPad) and 27 percent use the Android version (only available on Android phones). Another way Coop and his team push fans to the app is by posting a new celebration photo from the game on the app. He tweets it out at the end of the game to encourage folks to download the app.

Coop is pleased with the results so far. He told us…

We want our fans to be connected with the team as much as possible, and having an app allows us to have one more touch point that fans can be connected to. The app has many benefits over other ways fans can access information about the team, including push notifications, a visual presence on their device at all times and on optimized platform that can be accessed whether they are at the game or watching from home. We will continue to push for new features that are exclusive to the app or that are more easily accessible through the app so that the value of having the app increases for fans.

Coop is convinced that all brands should integrate their website, mobile, and social media sites. If they don't, they are missing out on fan and customer engagement that can help build their brand (Figures 4.9 and 4.10).

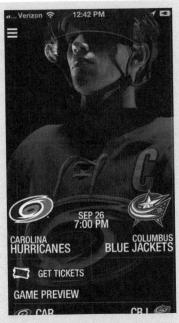

Figure 4.9 Home screen of the Carolina Hurricanes Official App for iOS

Figure 4.10 Game matchup details on the Carolina Hurricanes Official App for Android

Exercise to Learn Concepts

Here is a list, compiled by Mashable, of the 25 *Apps You'll Need to Survive College.*

How many of these apps have you tried? Of those, how do they make your life easier? Download one that you have not tried before and report back. Also, which apps are missing from this list?

Top Apps for College
BenchPrep
iStudiezPro
Evernote
StudyBlue Flashcards
RealCalc
Engineering Professional
EasyBib
Notella
Wolfram Alpha
Dictionary.com
Babylon.com
Jumpcut
Dragon Dictation
SelfControl
Studious
Circle of 6
Skype
LinkedIn
Twitter
Sworkit
Mint
Sleep if U can Alarm
Pocket first aid & CPR
Between
TED

Exercise to Apply Concepts

Think about the brand that you selected. What features would you expect their mobile app to have? How should they measure success?

Search for your favorite brand's app. Does it live up to your expectations? What is missing?

CHAPTER 5

Social Media Networks

Mobile Is Social and Social Is Mobile

Mobile phones were created to *facilitate communication*. Given our obsession with communicating over social media networks, it makes perfect sense that using social media on mobile devices is one of its most popular uses. According to comScore, 65 percent of time spent on social media networks happens on mobile.[1]

Some social networks, such as Facebook and LinkedIn, started on desktop screens but continuously see more usage from mobile devices. Other social networks, such as FourSquare and Instagram, started on mobile first. They may be viewable on desktop but these platforms were born from the mobile behaviors of capturing quick, on-the-go moments.

Regardless of the origin, these networks realize that their users expect to socialize anytime, anywhere, so they have taken steps to *optimize for mobile*, typically supporting native apps and mobile sites. This is great news for marketers. Apps and websites take time to plan, and build but getting started on social networks is as simple as opening an account and posting content.

Here is a look at which social networks U.S. owners are accessing from their phones (Figure 5.1):[2]

By far, Facebook has the most smartphone owners accessing it on a regular basis. However, this is based on all U.S. smartphone owners in the age group 13 and above. These percentages likely fluctuate if you just look at teens or just moms. Although it is easy to experiment with new *social platforms*, with so many networks out there, marketers need to be mindful that creating content and joining conversations on social networks does take time and money. Often times, marketers have to prioritize the platforms where their audience is most likely to be and start there.

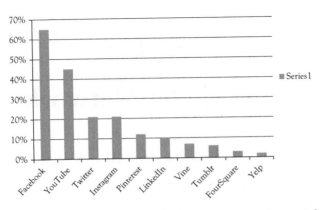

Figure 5.1 Percent of U.S. smartphone owners accessing social networks (Comscore December 2013)

Fifty-nine percent of social media users follow specific brands, however, *why* they follow brands varies.[3] They may follow a brand to show their support for a campaign, access coupons, get insider information, or just flag the brand as something they support. Marketers treat *Fans and Follows* just as they would a customer relationship database. This is a group of *super fans* that expect timely, relevant content. In return, brands strive for fans to socialize about their brand. Nielsen released a global study that revealed that peer recommendations are the most trusted form of advertising.[4] In addition, the Edelman Trust Barometer of 2014 confirms that 62 percent of consumers trust *a person like me*, third in line to academic or technical experts.* To facilitate this word-of-mouth marketing, brands focus their social feeds on sparking conversations. The more the brand can get customers to socialize with them, the more impressions or reach they will have, because engaging with a brand will post to a customer's followers.

A good example of this is how Burt's Bees is experimenting with Vine to show off its product in bite-sized bits (Figure 5.2).[5] The cosmetics brand launched #6SecondClassics, an effort that casts its classic products in roles in classic literature. It was Burt's Bees' first Vine campaign and

---

* http://www.scribd.com/fullscreen/200429962?access_key=key-25qv8l25jezgs6 th4bfc&allow_share=true&escape=false&show_recommendations= false&view_ mode=scroll

Figure 5.2 *Burt's Bees' Vine post*

included seven such videos on Little Women, 20,000 Leagues Under the Sea, Gulliver's Travels, Metamorphosis, Moby Dick, The Scarlet Letter, and Julius Caesar. The fun videos do not push product facts in your face. Instead, they are meant to spark a reaction, whether that is a *like*, a *re-Vine*, or an offline conversation about the cleverness of the campaign.

In addition to posting content, brands must always be listening and reacting to customer feedback, fostering *two-way conversations*. Many customers like airing their frustrations to their followers and are starting to expect brands to respond in that channel as well. In fact, 83 percent of Twitter users expect a same day customer service response.[6] Brands are working to accommodate this new demand. In a recent Forbes magazine article, American Airlines revealed that they now have 17 employees dedicated to social customer service, four focused on brand engagement and one working on social media measurement and reporting.[7]

Broadening Your Audience

Outside of a marketer's fans and friends of fans, there are many other social media users who might be interested in content from this marketer. To broaden its reach, many brands are tapping into advertising opportunities on mobile. As person browses their social media feed, they may see branded content that is sponsored or promoted. This means the brand is paying for the placement, in hopes that the person will take action based on the posted content. Once a person follows a brand, similar to customer relationship management (CRM), they will continue to receive branded content. Given how cluttered our e-mail inboxes have become, *social CRM* is a huge opportunity to remain in communication with customers. Look for more on social mobile advertisements in Chapter 6.

Publishing Mobile-Friendly Content

When leveraging social media, there is no separate experience for desktop and mobile. It is one feed, so marketers need to be mindful of how their customers will be engaging with it. *Visual storytelling* has become the norm so most posts typically have a high-resolution visual that accompanies it.

However, when it comes to video posts, the shorter the better for the mobile audience. Although mobile networks are getting stronger and many devices are connected to a Wi-Fi network when browsing content, it is much better to show a 15-second video than leave your audience trying to load a three-minute video on a slow connection.

For posts that include a link to a website, test the link on mobile to ensure the content will load. This goes back to Chapter 3 and the importance of a mobile web presence. If customers are on a mobile device and click through to a site that is not mobile optimized, they will be frustrated and may not return to your site going forward.

Measuring Success

Measuring social media efforts is the same from desktop to mobile. Depending on your goals, some measure success based on how many Fans and Followers they have and by how much those fans are engaging (i.e., commenting, liking, sharing, re-tweeting, tweeting with a brand's hashtag, re-pinning, and more). The more actions that are done, the more a brand's content is shared into others' feeds, blogs, boards, and more. Not only are these *earned impressions* important for returns on investment, but social media sharing is also excellent for search engine optimization.

Marketers will track any URL click-throughs from social posts to look for sales funnel activity such as searching for more information, adding to cart, and even purchasing. Additionally, many brands have access to social listening tools that help them monitor and nurture conversations surrounding their brand as well as gauge overall sentiment.

As with leveraging social media on desktop web, measuring social media effectiveness can be challenging. Seeing a friend of mine Tweet or Instagram a photo of a new product might plant a seed in my mind but when I later purchase that product in-store, does the retailer attribute my purchase to their social media presence, their in-store display, or other digital channels that I might have used in the shopping journey? Many marketers are working to better measure their social media presence and are documenting their findings on websites such as Social-MediaExaminer.com.

Case Study—Mercedes-Benz USA Take the Wheel Contest

During the summer of 2013, Mercedes-Benz wanted to introduce the new CLA-Class of cars to a younger demographic than they typically cater to. To reach this younger, digitally savvy car buyer, the brand hosted the Take the Wheel contest, which invited five of the top photographers on Instagram to spend five days behind the wheel of the all-new 2014 Mercedes-Benz CLA capturing images of their experiences. The photographer with the most likes, Chris Ozer with 478,951 likes during his week behind the wheel, took the vehicle home on a three-year lease. In addition to Ozer's likes, the brand also benefitted from the Instagram likes from his competitors: Michael O'Neal (285,127 likes), Paul Octavious (263,515 likes), Tim Landis (285,176 likes), and Alice Gao (358,508 likes). The brand benefitted by bringing more prospective customers and awareness to itself.

Participation was not limited to Instagram likes for drivers. Others were invited to apply to win their very own 2014 Mercedes CLA by visiting CLATaketheWheel.com, where their Instagram feed serves as a profile. The prize vehicle will go to the participant whose feed best reflects the true spirit of the 2014 Mercedes CLA-Class.*

* http://mone.al/clatakethewheel

Exercise to Learn Concepts

Analyze your favorite brand to see if it has a cross-platform social media presence.

1. Look for your favorite brand on cross-platform social experiences such as Facebook, Twitter, YouTube, Pinterest, and Yelp
2. How do the experiences vary from desktop to mobile?
3. Can you make a purchase from any or all of these sites?
4. Does your brand encourage two-way conversation among social media sites?
5. Has your brand experimented with any mobile-specific social experiences such as Instagram, Vine, or SnapChat?
6. What can you conclude about your brand? Would consumers find value from their social feeds while on a mobile phone?

Exercise to Apply Concepts

Think about your brand. When and why might people use social channels to shop your brand?

For example, if you are working in an art gallery, you might consider building a fan base on Facebook to update them on news, events, and sales. Share pictures of new work on Instagram and Pinterest to garner interest and consider experimenting with Vine and YouTube to create fun videos of the pieces on display. Also spend time listening and responding to feedback on Yelp.

CHAPTER 6

Mobile Advertising

Mobile advertising is a subset of mobile marketing. It has been defined as "text- and graphic-based commercial messages that are sent to consumers via mobile devices."[1] These ads can appear in different formats such as banners and video (discussed later) and can be inserted across various mobile properties such as mobile-optimized websites, apps and games, and more. Many marketers expect mobile advertising to operate in a similar manner to online advertising, but they are quite different.

Mobile Advertising's Superpower

Mobile advertising has a notable superpower—*context*. It's been said that *content* is King but content on mobile is King Kong. For marketers, delivering their message to the right person, at the right time and at the right place is the Holy Grail. Broadcast advertising, such as TV, print, and radio, can cast your message out to a large audience, but reaching the right audience can be difficult and cost prohibitive. With digital media, such as online display ads, marketers can use targeting methods to reach both broad and narrow audiences. However, despite online advertising's ability to achieve narrow, targeted audiences, the marketer was limited to where the message is delivered—often while a person is online at home or at the office. Now that mobile devices, especially smartphones, are widely used, mobile advertising helps marketers deliver campaigns, also both broad and narrow audiences, wherever they may be. Its ability to capture a person's location and deliver ads on mobile in a timely, contextual way, unlike any other marketing channel. Thus, mobile is being used as a marketing vehicle more and more due to its ability to target customers effectively, personalize content, and provide an interactive environment for customers due to the nature of the device (Figure 6.1).[2]

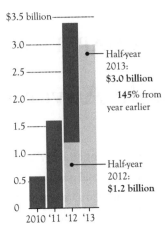

Figure 6.1 On the Go: U.S. mobile advertising revenue

Source: Chart retrieved from wsj.com*

---

* http://si.wsj.net/public/resources/images/MK-CJ674_FACEBO_G_20140129
190005.jpg

Today, according to Mary Meeker's latest study for KPCB, advertisers in the United States are spending approximately $7.1 billion per year on mobile advertising. Based on the amount of time we spend on our mobile phones, this is a small amount compared with what is being spent on other marketing channels such as TV, print, and radio. For example, the study shows that advertisers are spending 19 percent of their dollars on print advertising, whereas consumers are only spending 5 percent of their time there. Yet, while consumers spend an equivalent 20 percent of their time on their mobile phones, advertisers are only allocating 4 percent of their budget on mobile.[3] Mobile ad spending is estimated to be a $30 billion opportunity in the United States, once the market catches up[4] and begins to see return on investment (ROI) for this new medium.

Within the mobile advertising budget, search advertising captures about half of all global spending, most of which goes to Google, the most popular mobile search engine. As such, a large part of Chapter 3 was dedicated to covering the importance of search advertising, utilizing different search ad extensions and ensuring that the postclick experience is optimized for the searcher. Display advertisements account for approximately 45 percent of mobile ads spend, according to eMarketer[5] and are the main focus in this chapter. The remaining mobile ad share is claimed by messaging and e-mail ads.

Using Mobile Display

Under the umbrella of *mobile display*, marketers can use several types of ads to reach consumers on mobile. They include banner, interstitial, rich media, social, video, and sponsorship ads. Each is detailed below but as you see, there are various levels of creative and functional complexities.

Although marketers were able to synthesize online display ads into standard types and sizes, mobile marketers have not yet achieved this and it's not likely to happen any time soon. The challenge is that there are thousands of different devices with different applications and browsers. The Internet Advertising Bureau (IAB) and the Mobile Marketing Association (MMA) have published *Mobile Phone Creative Guidelines*[6] in effort to guide publishers on basic *standardization*. However, serving up a creative ad unit will never look great, or even good, on every device, so industry standardization is technically impossible.

Another thing to know is that display ad types perform differently depending on the publisher, or mobile site, or app that's displaying the ad. For example, what works on the Weather Channel app is not necessarily the best ad format for YouTube. With the Weather Channel, a person might be quickly looking up their daily forecast on weather.com and may not be open to a 15-second video clip. Alternatively, a YouTube viewer, who is watching several videos and open to be entertained, may be interested in a short, entertaining video ad.

The mobile display ecosystem is quite fragmented, so for marketers who want to test various ad units, across various audiences and across many publishers, creating and testing the ads can quickly become time and resource limiting. Often times, you'll see brands re-purpose TV spots in place of a mobile video ad, or you may see online banners resized for mobile. Everyone agrees that a more tailored experience will improve effectiveness but in the meantime, developing and deploying ads has proved harder than expected.

Using Standard Banners

Mobile banners, or *standard display ads*, are the most commonly used ad format.[7] Banner ads have traditionally been used to "convey an advertising/marketing message and/or encourage user to take an action."[8] Because so many brands and publishers have gone mobile, inventory is plentiful, and there are many creative sizes and formats to choose from.

Here is an example (Figures 6.2a and b) of how the CNN mobile app uses standard mobile display ads. The example at the bottom of this page is a standard banner and the one at the top of the next page is a large-sized banner.

The Forbes.com mobile website also uses banner advertising, although they use an *adhesion banner* to engage readers along the bottom of the site without disrupting the browsing experience (Figure 6.3). At the moment, adhesion banners are extremely popular among U.S. mobile website publishers, because the ads are scroll-proof, remaining above the fold of the page.

Figure 6.2a CNN standard banner ad; CNN iOS App

Figure 6.2b CNN large-sized banner ad; CNN iOS App

Figure 6.3 Adhesion banner on Forbes.com

Interstitial Banners

Standard banners are displayed alongside the browsing experience and can either be static or interactive (clickable). Interstitial banners, on the other hand, require a user to take action or close the ad, to continue their mobile experience.

Interstitial ads, or interstitials, can be static or interactive and serve an image or a video. Most commonly, you'll find interstitial ads appearing in between game turns, as you can see from the Tiny Pets advertisement in Figure 6.4. In this instance, the mobile gamer needed to either download the advertised app or click the x button to continue their game. The second example given in Figure 6.5 is an interstitial that appears within the USWeekly.com mobile site. This YouTube ad was served within an U.S. Weekly photo gallery so the viewer was required to engage or swipe

Figure 6.4 Tiny Pets ad

Figure 6.5 USMagazine.com on mobile

through the ad to continue viewing more photos. This uses the swipe gesture, making it very native to the photo gallery browsing experience.

Rich Media Ads—Expandables, Skins, and More

Rich media ads are highly engaging mobile ad experiences that allow a person to interact in a variety of ways. Depending on the creative used, a person can expand an ad or image, resize it, swipe or tap, snap a picture, and more. Often times, developers device functionalities such as the microphone, to serve these experiences.

Expandable banners, or expandables, allow a person to click on a standard-size banner to expand to reveal a full screen, rich media experience. These units do not take users away from their experience. Rather, they expand over the current page. Within the large, expanded unit, advertisers can offer click-to-play videos, swipeable image galleries, and functions that enable social sharing, e-mailing, texting, and even *mCommerce*.

The following example, from Walgreens, is an expandable that allows viewers to tap a banner to expand to full size. From there, they can wipe the chalkboard clean by swiping the phone screen and then interact with various product deals, take a quiz, locate a Walgreens store, or share the deal with friends on social media (Figures 6.6a, b, and c).

In addition to expandables, other rich media units can include a *site or app skin*, mini games, virtual photo booths, and other immersive experiences. Pandora uses audio ads in between streaming songs but may also display a banner while the audio ad is playing, in case a listener wants to take action. Toyota even used voice input technology to power a recent campaign to show off Corolla's new voice recognition system.[9]

The following three examples, all executed by Kargo, show rich mobile ads such as an animated site skin for Kraft on ET.com, a share-to-social feature for

Figure 6.6a Walgreens banner ad

Figure 6.6b Walgreens full size mobile screen

Figure 6.6c Walgreens product details

Source: Retrieved from: http://www.celtra.com/gallery

Garnier Fructis on Radar.com, and an interactive recipe finder on the Country Crock example (for site and app skin examples see Figures 6.7a, b, and c).

Rich media ads are becoming more popular among marketers, especially for raising brand awareness. As interactive as they are, the ads still offer control to the user to engage with as much or as little as they would like. Research studies have shown that interactive ads produce more favorable results with consumers.[10] For instance, one study found that when consumers have an opportunity to interact with the brand in a convenient way (e.g., click to get a free music file), they have a more favorable attitude toward the ad, the brand, and with an intention to purchase the brand.

Figure 6.7a Animated site skin for Kraft on ET.com—Site or app skin examples

Source: Retrieved from kargo.com*

---

* http://www.kargo.com/kargo-breakthrough-units/

Figure 6.7b A share-to-social feature for Garnier Fructis on Radar. com—Site or app skin examples

Source: Retrieved from kargo.com*

---

* http://www.kargo.com/kargo-breakthrough-units/

Additionally, the Interactive Advertising Bureau (IAB) introduced five new mobile ad formats called the Mobile Rising Stars. These new units, unlike proprietary publisher ad units, are designed to scale across many mobile web and app experiences. We have included links to the Mobile Rising Stars and mobile advertising guidelines in the Chapter 8 references.

Native Ads

Many high-trafficked publishers, such as Yahoo, Buzzfeed, and the Weather Channel, are releasing their own ad formats that integrate into their mobile experience in a more native, streamlined way. Think

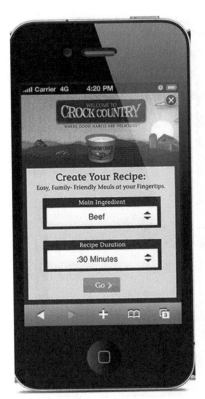

Figure 6.7c An interactive recipe finder on the Country Crock example—Site or app skin examples

Source: Retrieved from kargo.com*

---

* http://www.kargo.com/kargo-breakthrough-units/

Facebook promoted posts within your Newsfeed. These integrated ads can outperform standard units, but they are not for all advertisers, but custom creative assets are typically required.

Figures 6.8 to 6.10 show three examples of *native ads*. Figure 6.8 shows an editorial integration to download the Coupons.com mobile app within the Yahoo news feed. Buzzfeed, Figure 6.9, offers advertisers the opportunity to sponsor content. In this example, a news story is promoted by Fuze. The Weather Channel app, Figure 6.10, offers full-screen advertisements that are designed around the site and app's template to appear natural and integrated, as this Kellogg's ad does.

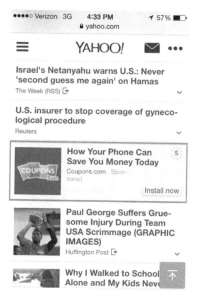

Figure 6.8 An editorial integration to download the Coupons.com mobile app within the Yahoo news feed

Source: Retrieved from Yahoo.com

Figure 6.9 Buzzfeed offers advertisers the opportunity to sponsor content

Source: Retrieved from Buzzfeed.com

Figure 6.10 The Weather Channel app offers full-screen advertisements that are designed around the site and app's template to appear natural and integrated, as this Kellogg's ad does

Source: Retrieved from CreativeBloq.com*

---

* http://media.creativebloq.futurecdn.net/sites/creativebloq.com/files/images /2014/05/weather3.jpg

Serving Ads on Social Media

As we shared in Chapter 5, according to comScore, 65 percent of time spent on social media happens on mobile. Not only is it important to socialize with fans and customers on these channels but there is also an opportunity to broaden your reach and acquire new customers through social. These ads, sometimes called *social mobile ads*, are wildly popular and being served native to the platform, similar to what we just saw from Yahoo, Buzzfeed, and the Weather Channel.

Twitter started the native-social ad trend with Promoted Tweets in early 2010.[11] Today, mobile contributes 80 percent to Twitter's total ad revenue.[12] In the shadow of Twitter, when Facebook shareholders raised concern with stock prices in June 2013, Mark Zuckerberg turned his strategy to mobile advertising, which was accounting for 30 percent of Facebook's ad revenue at the time.[13] One year later, Facebook reports that mobile now accounts for approximately 62 percent of their ad revenue.[14]

Seeing these strong financials, other social networks, such as Foursquare, Instagram, and Pinterest are quickly rolling out or piloting mobile ads on their platforms. Expect to see major growth and innovation in mobile social ads in the near future. In the meantime, here is a look at a few mobile social native ads (Figures 6.11 to 6.13).

Figure 6.11 Twitter Promoted Tweet

Source: Retrieved from Twitter app.

Figure 6.12 Facebook Sponsored Page Post

Source: Retrieved from Facebook app.

Figure 6.13 Instagram Sponsored Photo

Source: Retrieved from Instagram app.

Using Video Ads

Available on social networks or other sites and apps, with faster mobile data speeds, video is finally a reality for mobile marketers. Whether it is a *preroll ad* before watching a show on Hulu's mobile app or a TV commercial imbedded in a news app, a new MMA study reports that 75 percent of *video ads* are served within apps. Video ads can vary in length from a few seconds to a minute but the recent study shows that users are most likely to click after watching a medium length video between 15 and 30 seconds, versus under 15 seconds or over 30 seconds.[15] Some video ads might allow the user to skip it but the study goes on to report that so long as they are not fatigued by too many video ads, nonskip ads typically see very high completion rates (over 90 percent).

Videos work hard to raise awareness, but to engage viewers some advertisers choose to include an overlay or an end card to offer additional engagement. These can include various calls-to-action such as *tap to learn more* or *buy it now*, and they provide that interactive conversion element to the ads.

Here are two examples (Figures 6.14 and 6.15) of video ads. The mobile video ad show in Figure 6.14, playing on YouTube, is from Ortho with an option on the top right to click through and visit the brand. The mobile video ad in Figure 6.15 is a Scion end card, which allows the person to watch another video or build their own FR-S car.

Figure 6.14 Ortho ad on YouTube.com

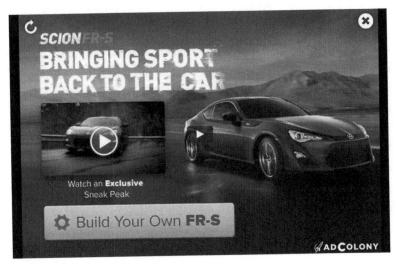

Figure 6.15 Scion video end card

Source: Retrieved from http://www.adcolony.com/brands/endcards/

Sponsorships

Brands can also look to *mobile sponsorships* to reach groups of targeted consumers that are engaged and interacting with the app or site on a daily basis. Sponsorships are especially popular for sports, entertainment, and event apps where consumers have similar traits, making message targeting simple for advertisers.

One example is from Unilever's Axe, who was the launch sponsor of Comedy Central's CC: Stand-Up app, which pulls in video content from over 700 comedians. Axe integrated into the experience by curating a playlist of eight sponsored videos called *Laugh Your Face Off* and ran pre-roll video ads throughout the app experience. Engaging with the ads took app users to a landing page where they could read reviews and learn more about Axe products. Knowing that both Comedy Central and Axe target young, heavily social men, the partnership was a perfect way to expose Axe to the Comedy Central app audience (Figures 6.16 and 6.17).[16]

Similarly, Jack Link's Beef Jerky partnered with sports app, theScore, to sponsor baseball coverage in August 2013. The integrated included customized baseball-themed content, such as *Snackable Facts*, delivered via dynamic banners and 60-second videos. "Partnering with the Score

Figure 6.16 Axe sponsorship with Comedy Central Stand-Up app

Source: Retrieved from MobileMarketer.com*

---

* http://www.mobilemarketer.com/cms/lib/17499.jpg

Figure 6.17 Jack Link's sponsorship within theScore's app

Source: Retrieved from MobileMarketer.com*

---

* http://www.mobilemarketer.com/cms/lib/18272.jpg

was a natural fit for Jack Link's," said Kevin Papacek, director of marketing for Jack Link's. "We love to help sports fans 'Feed Their Wild Side' with custom content that's only available with this platform."[17]

Targeting on Mobile

Now that you are familiar with the different mobile ad formats and creative opportunities, the focus turns to how to deliver that message most effectively.

To reach the right audience, mobile advertisers can target predetermined audience profiles (young men, moms, and others) or can create custom profiles based on their brand. Inputs can include age, gender, household income, education, as well as sites visited, ads clicked, purchased items, car make and model, and more.

By overlaying these audiences on to intent and interest data, advertisers can reach in-market mobile consumers across verticals such as auto, travel, shopping, gardening, technology, entertainment, finance, and more. By integrating first-party and third-party data sources, mobile platforms in the space offer advertisers a scaled reach with strong insights that help show the strongest results. Rest assured that audience data are privacy protected.

Another key way to target audiences on mobile is based on location, which can add context to the message, especially when someone is out and about. *Location-based advertising* seems to carry a lot of hype but it is just in its infancy, compared with other targeting tactics. One of the main reasons that marketers have not invested more in location-based marketing is the inefficiency of gathering accurate mobile location data. If an advertiser can get a person's permission to capture their latitude and longitude (lat/long), the ad can be geo-fenced based on a local business or competitor's business. However, not all publishers ask for a person's location, which can disrupt the browsing experience. Or, people decline to share their location. This quickly drives up price.

Instead, many location-based advertisers are being presented with a *cocktail* of data from other location inputs such as Wi-Fi, GPS, cell phone tower triangulation, IP location detection, designated market area, and more.[18] These methods can infer location and drive scale but true lat/long

Figure 6.18 *Jack in the Box ad within The Weather Channel app*
Source: Retrieved from ThinkNear.com*

---

* http://www.thinknear.com/solutions.html

is the only precise method available, outside of methods such as low-energy Bluetooth, or iBeacon marketing, which is discussed in Chapter 7. Despite the challenges, inferred location targeting can be highly effective for brands. Location-based experts, Placed, have helped early adopters see double-digit gains in click-through rate (CTR), conversion rate, and targetable inventory.* Figure 6.18 shows an example of how a location-based mobile banner might look and act depending on its proximity to a restaurant.

It is important to note that targeting on mobile has additional layers of complexity so the methods differ a bit from desktop targeting. Features such as *retargeting* and *frequency capping* do not apply or work in the same way on mobile, largely because *cookies* do not work in iPhone apps. If your campaign runs only on Android or mobile web, cookies may work—but only if they are *first-party cookies*. New and better ways of tracking and serving ads across devices are in development but in the meantime, mobile targeting remains much less powerful than desktop targeting.[19]

---

* https://www.placed.com/targeting

The good news for advertisers is that consumers are willing to be targeted with ads on their mobile phones. This is a major hurdle for mobile advertising effectiveness: *consumer permission*. A JWire survey (2010) found that smartphone users not only responded to advertising on apps, but made a purchase as a result. In addition, these consumers were receptive to being sent location-based ads.[20]

Streamlining Mobile Ad Planning and Buying

Given that an identified audience likely frequents a variety of mobile experiences, advertisers are constantly looking for efficiencies of how to find their audiences across all of these touch points. Enter *programmatic buying*.

This method of real-time optimization to reach audiences is reshaping the entire digital advertising landscape. These platforms are automating much of the ad buying and selling process and increasing the accuracy of execution. Although there are some barriers to adoption, the industry is seeing a massive uptick in programmatic and *real-time bidding* (RTB) on desktop and the shift is quickly proliferating on mobile, as well.[21]

Measuring Success

As with desktop display advertising, brands are working to better understand the ROI in mobile advertising. Cost per mile (CPM) and CTR continue to be the leading benchmarks for gauging the effectiveness of mobile display. Neither metric is perfect but over time, tracking CPM and CTR rates can provide insight into the particular ad formats.

According to industry reports, such as eMarketer's *Mobile Advertising Scorecard*, mobile banners see very low CTRs, that is, average CTR for HTML5 mobile banners in 2013 was 11 percent. Due to slow connections, some banners go unserved. Or when served, people simply ignore them, as they became trained to do on desktop, over time. However, CTR is just one metric. Banners that are relevant, credible, and useful can also be effective[22]—especially for raising awareness for a brand.

According to a study by PointRoll, mobile rich media delivered over one third more brand time per interaction than desktop Rich Media in 2013. The study also found that rich media ads with embedded video generated five times the CTR of rich media ads without video.[23] And when it comes to rich media formats, the eMarketer report went on to reveal that expandables typically perform best, allowing the user to take control of the experience.

To measure these ads beyond the initial click, many marketers are starting to employ secondary metrics—such as engagement or interaction rate, completion rate, or time spent with the ad—in order to gauge performance. Video ads, for example, can be measured using CTR, start rate, and completion rate. Most marketers interviewed by eMarketer gave mobile in-stream video strong marks for effectiveness but the challenge is often low inventory, which can drive up cost.

By leveraging client data feeds or third-party research, mobile advertising effectiveness can also be measured by *door open rate, register ring rate, brand lift rate, product purchase rate,* and *screen jump rate,* to highlight a few of the Millennial Media's omni measurement solutions.*

One last thing to mention is the importance of an omni-channel strategy. A recent comScore study found that mobile sales increased by 119 percent when mobile consumers were exposed to both search and display ads for a retailer, as opposed to just display (16 percent) or just search (82 percent).[24] Their conclusion is that even mobile consumers respond to *multiple touch points* or an *integrated strategy* that provides them with a similar message in different contexts.[25]

Case Study: Pantene's Beautiful Hair Whatever the Weather[26]

Losing touch with consumers, facing massive competitive noise and realizing a sales decline, Arc Worldwide, Pantene's shopper marketing agency, needed to get Pantene back on the radar and into the shower. And they did so by solving a real problem for their target—weather-related bad hair days. Arc reframed existing products as solutions

---

* http://www.millennialmedia.com/advertise/measurement/

for any weather extreme in the place the customer checks the weather the most, The Weather Channel, across its mobile, tablet, and desktop properties. When the customer checked her forecast, she was served a geo-targeted haircast with the right Pantene product to match, and sent her shopping at her go-to destination for solving hair problems, Walgreens. In the end, the Pantene business was turned around at this key retailer and millions of women were given beautiful hair, whatever the weather.

This campaign effectively used *emotion*, a short-term feeling that drives behavior,[27] to gain the attention of its target market. A key insight for the campaign was that women do not blame the weather for bad hair; instead, she blames her hair products. Recent research found that a focus on emotions, such as anger, fear, joy, or sadness, can be an effective way to reach consumers.[28] And, in particular, a study with younger consumers showed that they displayed positive emotions when being shown a lighthearted or entertaining ad,[29] which is certainly the case here with a bad hair day!

Figure 6.19 Weather Channel/Pantene campaign mobile ad screens

Source: Retrieved from http://www.getelastic.com/wp-content/uploads/forecast-frizz-pantene.jpg

Below are examples of what shoppers might see when she views her local weather forecast on The Weather Channel. These full-screen ads were designed specifically for placement on The Weather Channel apps, deeming them native ads (Figure 6.19). They could also be considered a sponsorship. The interactive call to action *Find it at a Walgreens near you* brings richness to the media unit and quickly helps shoppers locate their nearest store (likely a key performance indicator, or KPI, for the campaign.)

Exercise to Learn Concepts

Analyze a publication on mobile (e.g., WIRED, Glamour, Fast Company) and identify any mobile advertising or sponsorships that you see.

1. Do the ads seem to be standard sized or more customized to the site or app?
2. Are they being used to generate awareness or do they have calls to action and conversion?
3. Is that publication a credible source for the brand?
4. What happens when you tap the ads?
5. Once you have tapped the ad, watched the video, or engaged with the experience, was it easy to return back to browsing?

Exercise to Apply Concepts

Think about your brand. Why might you want to use mobile advertising? What sites or apps would you want your ads to appear on? What types of ad units or formats would you use?

CHAPTER 7

Accessing Content

Knowing that brands use mobile as a channel to offer people always-on information and entertainment, there are various ways people will come across *branded content*. When people are in an active state—searching, browsing, and interacting—they will come across *pull tactics*. These tactics offer a presence to address people's needs as they arise. *Push tactics*, on the other hand, are used to spark activity. They often alert and sometimes interrupt, in an effort to drive engagement.

Pull Tactics

Common pull tactics include

- mobile-optimized website(s)
- mobile app(s)
- search engine optimization
- quick-response (QR) codes
- messaging (SMS/MMS/RMM)
- near-field communication (NFC).

Marketers often use a combination of pull tactics and communicate contextually relevant calls to action. For on-the-move radio listeners, a radio DJ might encourage listeners to text their song request versus log on to their website or send an e-mail. When it comes to in-store shopping, where some mobile phones receive poor reception, stores such as Target are encouraging guests to log on to their free in-store Wi-Fi to access the Target mobile apps, helping them get to their shopping lists and coupons. While browsing through a magazine, people might have more time to visit a website directly or use search to look up a product they like. Because you're already familiar with accessing content via web, app, and search, we'll focus now on how QR codes, SMS/MMS/RMM messaging, NFC, and other pull tactics work.

Using QR Codes as Quick Links to Content

QR codes, or quick-response codes, allow brands to link to digital content from a nondigital medium, such as a print ad. One important thing to note: people cannot just snap a picture of the code. Rather, a QR code or barcode reader app (e.g., Scanlife) must be downloaded and used to scan the code. Once scanned, the app will quickly redirect the person to a mobile website. Unfortunately, QR codes and other image recognition searches (such as Google Goggles, and SnapTags), have been slow to gain mass adoption.

The two biggest hurdles have been (1) lack of communication on *why* people should scan their code, and (2) *how* people can scan. Some marketers include a QR code on their advertising, but they forget to tell people *why* they should scan it and *how* they can scan it. Consumers end up with too many questions, such as Will it give me a deal? Will it take me to the app store to download your app? Also, will it save me time? If I can type in AmericanAirlines.com, I should not be expected to open an app and scan a code to reach this site. QR codes should only be used as a short cut or a deep link to content that would be otherwise difficult to find. For example, Home Depot deployed QR codes in its garden department to help shoppers easily understand the need for sunlight and water for plants and flowers (Figures 7.1 and 7.2). Rather than searching for each plant, the code provided a simple shortcut. This is a good use of QR codes.

The other issue with QR codes is that they are not alone—there are scanable barcodes, other brands of codes such as SnapTags, image search apps, and more. This disparate ecosystem is not easy to communicate to people. Some magazines expect shoppers to know that if they take a picture and e-mail a SnapTag, they can get more information. In the same magazine, a brand's print ad might instead have a standard QR code for readers to scan. In stores, apps such as RedLaser encourage shoppers to scan Universal Product Codes or UPC codes on products to find a better price or get more information.

With all of these unique solutions, it falls on the marketers to not only explain *why* to scan a code (the benefits) but also *how* to scan the code. In

Figure 7.1 Home Depot QR code example

Source: Retrieved from bustercreative.com*

---

* http://bustercreative.com/wp-content/uploads/2011/09/hd-Home-Depot-Interactive-Plant-Tags-Help-You-Learn-and-Save-Money-The-Home-Depot-Blog-.jpg

comparison, in other countries like China, these codes are standardized and most phones come preloaded with a barcode reader app. People know how to scan codes so marketers only need to communicate why scanning a code will add value.

While scanning adoption may be low in the United States, marketers can test this tactic if there's a need and easily track each code's scans. Appliances, for example, are very difficult to search for because they have long model numbers, often specific to certain stores. Recognizing this, Best Buy added QR codes to every product information tag in stores. That way, shoppers can quickly access the Best Buy product page to read ratings and reviews, compare the appliance to others similar to it, view warranties, and more. Shoppers can use a QR code reader to scan these codes or for additional benefit, they can even use the QR code reader embedded into the Best Buy app. This use of QR codes offers value so it's just up to Best Buy to easily communicate how to scan the codes to encourage strong results.

Figure 7.2 Home Depot QR codes on products

Source: Retrieved from imediaconnection.com*

---

* http://www.imediaconnection.com/images/content/120510_Cummings_14_
plants.jpg

Offer SMS/MMS/RMM to Access Content

Messaging can actually be used as a push pull tactic or both. As a pull
tactic, similar to QR codes, messaging can act as a way to link people
deeply to the content. Messages are routed back and forth using short
codes, which are like phone numbers but usually only four to six digits.

Easier to remember than a phone number, brands might like people to
text APP to 12345 to get their app. In this *call to action*, APP is considered
the campaign's *keyword* and 12345 is the *short code*. When a person sends

this text, they'll receive a reply back with more information, usually including a URL that they can click. In this instance, it saves the person from the need to search for this app in the app store. To watch a movie trailer, a poster might say text POWER to 45321. When a person sends the keyword POWER to the shortcode 45321, they may, in this case, receive an MMS or RMM back with a short video clip trailer (Figures 7.3 and 7.4).

Target has been driving shoppers to coupons by offering an SMS call to action in stores. In this example, GROCERY1 is the keyword and 827438. Pro tip: many smartphones will let you send a branded number (TARGET) instead of the actual short code (827438). This makes it even easier for a shopper to get to the coupon quickly.

Figure 7.3 Photo taken inside a Chicago, Illinois Target store showing an in-store text message call-to-action

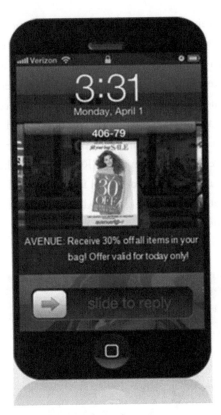

Figure 7.4 Example of RMM from Avenue

Source: Retrieved from marketingland.com*

---

* http://marketingland.com/wp-content/ml-loads/2014/01/Iris-Mobile-Mobile-Messaging-Image-300x451.png

Messaging is particularly useful for people using older phones (feature phones do not usually have data plans and are slow to load web pages.) Although these later adopters may be used to texting and occasionally loading a web page, it's not as common for them to search the web and because they cannot access apps, scanning a QR code is out of the question. As smartphone adoption continues to increase, it might be more common to see direct URL calls to action, image scanning, and so forth. Because messaging can get a bit expensive for marketers, as each message has a cost.

Testing Near-Field Communication

Many of the new Android smartphones coming out include a near-field communication *(NFC)-chip* embedded in the phones. Although this feature has just started to appear on devices, global NFC penetration is forecasted to rise to 64 percent in 2018.[1] NFC uses short-range high-frequency wireless communication to connect two devices and transfer data when they're within a short range. When the phone comes close or taps an NFC-enabled tag, a mobile site can load instantly, a mobile payment can be initiated, a video can be downloaded, and more. This is ideal for marketers because so long as the person has an NFC chip in their phone, with a simple tap, they can be shopping or buying on your site. NFC tags can be built into an experience or be applied like a sticker. Regardless, we've seen early NFC examples placed on in-store movie posters, bus shelters, public transit payment terminals, and even in magazines.

To promote their NFC-enabled smartphones, Samsung launched *Share to Go* kiosks in 2013, which offered Galaxy III owners free music downloads, videos, TV shows, and books (Figure 7.5). Passerby's simply

Figure 7.5 Samsung Share to Go kiosk

Source: Retrieved from hub.tappinn.com*

---

* http://hub.tappinn.com/blog/wp-content/uploads/2014/01/NFC-sign-poster.jpg

turned on their NFC functionality and waved their phone near the NFC tag to access the content. Similarly, Kraft tested NFC signs in grocery stores (Figure 7.6). Shoppers could tap their phones on the signs to see related recipes and ingredients for easy meal inspiration. This 2012 grocery store pilot *delivered 12 times the engagement level of QR codes.*[2]

This is an emerging tactic that has very low adoption—partially because it's so new and also in part because only some phones are offering this feature (notably, iPhone does not). Knowing that, it could be worth a test but only if a second call to action is included (text, scan, and so on) In fact, Kraft used *Tap or Snap* as a call to action to invite any smartphone users to their content.

Figure 7.6 Kraft NFC Pilot

Source: Retrieved from mobilemarketer.com*

---

* http://www.mobilemarketer.com/cms/lib/18078.jpg

Other Pull Tactics to Connect to Content

Image recognition is still advancing as engineers continue to improve bookmarking capabilities and databases of *image matching*. Amazon is placing big bets on image recognition with its Fire Smartphone feature called Firefly. By pressing and holding a dedicated button, the Fire Phone can recognize printed phone numbers, e-mail and web addresses, business cards, and much more. Firefly even works at a distance, so you can capture a phone number on a sign from across the street, for example.

Audio recognition has also made leaps of improvement in past years. Voice recognition services, such as Apple's Siri, are becoming a standard feature, helping people reach content by talking to their device, whether that's your phone or your glasses. That's right. Expect to see more people talking to themselves, or to their Google Glasses, as wearable devices begin to proliferate.[3]

Brands haven't done much in the way of promoting voice recognition to search for content but they have experimented with audio recognition through apps such as Shazam and SoundHound. These apps use the phone's microphone to listen to background noise, decode it, and present relevant content. Many people use the apps to listen to a song and identify the artist and title. However, with quick links to purchase content, savvy marketers have tested these apps in other ways. Old Navy, for example, included the Shazam logo on their TV ads, encouraging *on the couch* shoppers to listen to the ad to instantly shop the clothes and accessories featured in the spot. This second screen experience is a smart way to connect people with digital content but, similar to scanning QR codes, you have to open a particular app to access content. Also, these apps need to capture approximately 10 seconds of audio to identify what it hears. Knowing it will take a few seconds to unlock the phone and open the app, Shazam-able ads should only be used in advertisements that are at least 30 seconds long, whether that's a TV spot or another type of ad platform.

Another exciting way to use apps to serve content is using *augmented reality (AR) technology*. When a person uses an AR-powered app and looks through the camera lens, a layer of information is placed on screen to reveal beneficial details in the form of visual data imagery layered on top that are not normally visible.

The Yelp app has an augmented reality feature called *Monocle*, which displays search results and its ratings based on where you're standing (Figure 7.7). Ikea's 2014 catalog app uses AR to allow shoppers to preview how furnishings will look in their home before buying. After selecting an item from the app, Ikea places a special graphic symbol in the spot where they want to see the item and point their phone to view how it will look within the current environment (Figure 7.8). Although AR can add a fun, exciting way to view data, it can be a bit cumbersome to use. Look for better and better experiences as phones continue to improve processing speeds and location accuracy.

Push Tactics

The opposite of pull tactics, push tactics are used to remind, invite, or spark an interaction. In addition to e-mail that was discussed in Chapter 2 and mobile display that was discussed in Chapter 6, push tactics include the following:

Figure 7.7 Example of Yelp's Monocle feature

Source: Retrieved from neww.medill.northwestern.edu*

---

* http://news.medill.northwestern.edu/uploadedImages/News/Chicago/Images/ Science/aug_yelp.jpg

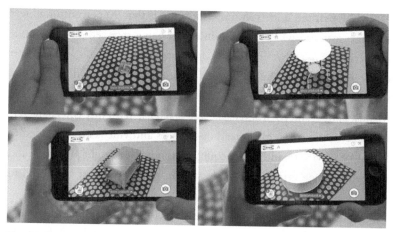

Figure 7.8 Example of IKEA's augmented reality catalog
Source: Retrieved from 1.design-milk.com*

---

* http://1.design-milk.com/images/2013/08/IKEA-augmented-reality-app-cata-logue-05-600x331.jpg

- SMS/MMS/RMM
- App push notifications
- iBeacon messages.

To capture a mobile user's attention, marketers typically use one or more push tactics. However, because they may interrupt a person, it's critical to be contextually relevant. That means using judgment about when and where a person will be when they receive the message. For example, sending a text message late at night will surely not get the response you're looking for.

Using SMS/MMS/RMM to Push Content

Text and rich messages push to phones just as e-mails do. Both are database marketing tools with segmentation opportunities but consumers treat text messages in a more personal and immediate way. As mentioned earlier, a recent SinglePoint study found that text message open rates exceed 99 percent, and even more shocking is that 90 percent of all text messages are read within three minutes of being received on the mobile phone. *That's nearly three times the open rate of most e-mail messages.*[4] Part of the reason is that the message is reaching a captive audience. When we receive a text, we often look at it immediately because many of our friends, family, and co-workers use it to reach us. With just 160 characters available, texts offer a quick read but images and videos can be added to RMM or MMS, to add visual equity. Although we might allow a brand we love to come into this message stream, marketers must be careful to respect a mobile user's privacy and time.

Organizations such as the Mobile Marketing Association (MMA) and mobile carriers have taken careful measures to ensure mobile inboxes do not become spam repositories, the way e-mail inboxes have become. If a person shares their mobile phone number with a brand, it does not mean the brand has an open invitation to begin sending text messages to this customer. Instead, brands need to *ask permission* to send SMS, MMS, and RMM messages using a double opt-in process that requires customers to reply with an affirmative keyword (e.g., YES) to confirm that they are willing to receive ongoing messages.

Once a consumer opts-in from ongoing alerts, marketers will also want to be mindful of how frequently they send a message, the day and time the message will be sent and what content is included. Some marketers such as airlines, pharmacies, and banks focus on time-sensitive alerts, for instance, if there is a flight gate change, a prescription ready, or a low account balance. Other marketers such as retailers and restaurants send SMS, MMS, and RMM messages to drive traffic with deals, offers, and exclusive news. They may even leverage location-based services to send messages only when you are within a certain distance from their store or a competitor's store. As mentioned in Chapter 2, this is called geo-fencing.

Regardless of the use case, it's critical for marketers to follow the Mobile Marketing Association (MMA) double opt-in guidelines to ensure they are complaint with consumer best practices. Look for a link to the guidelines in Chapter 8.

Driving App Engagement with Push Notifications

Marketers with a mobile app have the opportunity to ask users if they would like to receive Push Notifications. These notifications are meant to drive users back into the app to buy or consume more content. With even fewer characters available than SMS messages and without the ability to include images and video, these pushes are very simple but can be segmented geo-targeted based on a person's location.

Similar to an SMS/MMS/RMM opt-in, once a user has opted in, you don't want to overwhelm them with too many messages. This might cause a person to not just opt out of push notifications, but they might also delete your app altogether. To avoid this, app marketers should use good judgment on when and why to push app notifications. For time-sensitive notifications, such as a breaking news story or a friend's nearby social media check-in, time is critical so the message is pushed immediately. For less urgent content, such as gaming or new app feature announcements, marketers schedule these pushes for days or times that users will be most likely to respond.

Done right, research from Urban Airship shows daily app usage increasing by up to 540 percent with push notifications.[5] However, with people downloading more and more apps, allowing push notifications may become less likely due to clutter. By offering value and a reason to accept app push notifications, users may be more inclined to opt-in and remain subscribed (Figures 7.9 and 7.10).

Engaging App Users with iBeacon Technology

Location-based services are getting more accurate, especially when a mobile user is on Wi-Fi, but other technologies, such as iBeacon, are offering pushes using Bluetooth technology when an app user is within distance to a beacon. This is an especially good solution when people are indoors where cell phone signals may be blocked, making GPS coordinates difficult or impossible to locate. Beacons are low-cost pieces of hardware, small enough to be hidden on a store shelf or attached to a wall. They use battery-friendly, low-energy Bluetooth transmissions and when it locates

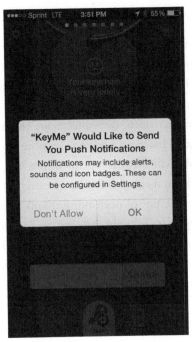

Figure 7.9 Example of KeyMe iOS app asking for Push Notification opt in

a nearby phone, it will push open a specified mobile app so long as it's installed on the person's phone.

iBeacon technology is new and is currently being piloted by many retailers. For example, in December 2013, Apple Stores enabled iBeacon location-aware transmitters at all of its U.S. retail stores, giving the company the ability to easily provide product information and allow shoppers to quickly check out via their iPhone. When shoppers with the Apple Store app entered the store, a splash screen came up telling them about the functionality and asks if the shopper will agree to receive in-store notifications (Figure 7.11). From there, geo-fencing would begin to track their location and push messages when they come within a beacon. One message was *Shopping for accessories? Read product reviews and make your purchase right from your iPhone.*

Performance data has not yet validated whether or not this tactic is effective but many marketers think that this could be effective for in-aisle promotions and other location-sensitive messaging.

Figure 7.10 Example of CNN and Blitz iOS push notifications

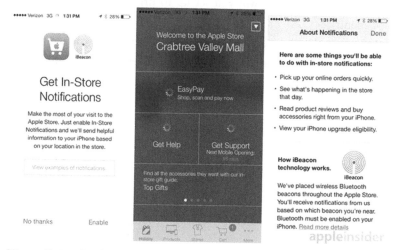

Figure 7.11 Apple's use of Geo-fencing to request pushing in-store notifications

Source: Retrieved from cdn1.appleinsider.com*

---

* http://cdn1.appleinsider.com/store-131206-1.jpg

Exercise to Learn Concepts

Analyze your favorite brand to see which pull and push tactics they offer to mobile users.

1. Which pull tactics are offered? (Mobile site, app, search, and so on)
2. Have you seen any print or in-store signs that offer QR codes or other pull mobile calls-to-action?
3. Which push tactics are offered? (E-mail, SMS/MMS/RMM alerts, app push notifications, and others)
4. Have you seen any print or in-store signs that mention signing up for push messaging?

Exercise to Apply Concepts

Imagine that you've created an interactive map mobile app for prospective students and visitors.

1. List pull tactics to get visitors to download the app.
2. Which push tactics will you set up to drive ongoing app engagement?
3. For people who may not use a smartphone, how could you use text messaging to teach people about different buildings and sights around campus?

CHAPTER 8

Mobile Marketing Strategy and Resources

After learning the importance and relevance of mobile marketing and the different tactics available to deploy, it's time for you to start building your brand's strategy for mobile. There are several inputs that go into establishing a strategy and each could take marketers months to fine tune. However, knowing this channel is moving quickly, time is of the essence. Look for ways to have quick wins that align with a longer-term vision.

To get to a longer-term vision, try using the *N.O.T.E. framework** to get started.

Needs	Determine what your customers need by: • Conducting research • Identifying trends, data and insights from current digital properties
Objectives	Prioritize those customer needs based on your business objectives: • Set short-term goals • Establish a long-term vision
Tactics	Identify the best tactics to achieve customer needs and business objectives: • Generate feature lists and choose the most appropriate tactics for your customers • Work towards building a foundation for ongoing communication
Execution	Document an action plan • Create a roadmap to prioritize efforts based on cost, timing and importance • Establish success metrics • Tell customers about your new mobile programs and optimize

---

* Molly Garris

Understanding the N.O.T.E. Framework

To illustrate how to use the framework, let's apply it to a fictitious client—an ice cream shop.

Needs: Start by surveying current customers and friends about what they might need or expect from your ice cream shop on mobile. Make a list of these needs and ask them to tell you what would be most important. Research what your competitors do—what's working for them and what could be improved? Consider other trends and take a look at your existing digital properties. From your *website analytics*, what percentage of visits come from mobile devices? Which platforms (iOS, Android, and others) are they on? From e-mail analytics, how many opens come from mobile? What about search?

Objectives: Next, think what business objectives you'd like to address with mobile. Whether it's to upsell customers, get more traffic to the store, urge people to try new products or flavors, or to build loyalty, prioritize customer needs with your business goals in mind.

Tactics: Now that you have an understanding of what you need to accomplish, balancing customer needs with objectives, consider the right tactics to use to bring these features to life. Let's say that one of the features is providing shop hours and think back to the tactics we covered. Would your customers search for shop hours? Would they potentially go to your website on mobile to find hours? Would there be a need for an app for this? Would customers seek out shop hours on social media networks? Would you use mobile display to promote the ice cream shop hours? Would store hours be a feature that customers would want pushed to them via e-mail, messaging, or other tactic?

Also, take into consideration which behaviors your customer does on mobile. Are they smartphone-savvy? Do cell phones typically have coverage in your shop? If not, is there Wi-Fi? How will you tell customers about your new mobile program? How could you ask to stay in touch with them on an ongoing basis?

Execution: Before actioning tactics, to action tactics, set a plan in place. This is an especially good time to bring in mobile agencies or specialists for consultation, if you haven't already. Many marketers create roadmaps to organize features, tactics, cost of each, timing to develop each, and how these are prioritized for short and long term. Then, generate a measurement plan for each tactic to benchmark progress. Once you begin building or executing the tactics, make time to monitor the analytics. Look for areas to optimize and improve. Digital marketing is iterative and constantly improving to continue serving today's connected customers.

Applying the N.O.T.E. Framework

Here's how we applied the N.O.T.E. framework to our fictitious ice cream shop.

Needs: After completing this exercise, our customers want to use their phones to find out the store hours, address or location, and featured flavors. They also want to view e-mails, which include featured flavors on mobile, and use the loyalty card program from their device. One customer mentioned a loyalty app from a frozen yogurt brand so that prompted us to do competitive research to see how it worked and what other frozen treat brands were doing on mobile. Our Google Analytics showed that 55 percent of website visits came from mobile. We also learned that our customers love social media, especially visual platforms such as Facebook, Instagram, SnapChat, and Vine.

Objectives: We know that once people come to the ice cream shop, they are easily cross-sold and up-sold. They are also happy with the experience and willing to return. Our focus on mobile will be acquiring new customers to come into the store and getting current customers to evangelize our business.

Tactics: We're planning to build a mobile-optimized website to support existing and prospective customers by offering store hours, address or location, and featured flavors. We also hope to appeal to new customers by including reviews from existing customers. To drive traffic to the site, we'll use location-based mobile display ads during spring and summertime to encourage people to visit the ice cream shop. We'll also begin posting images to Facebook and Instagram of featured flavors and ask fans to like or share these posts.

Execution: Because social media is free to use, we will start posting content several times per week right away. In-store signs will be created to invite loyal customers to share their photos with #icecreamshoplove and leave reviews on Yelp. Our goal will be to obtain 1,000 followers on Facebook and Instagram.

We'll also capture at least 10 text and video testimonials from our most frequent customers to post on social media and on our website, with their permission of course.

At the same time, we'll begin building our mobile website, ensuring it's optimized for *search engine marketing*. We'll get early customer feedback from a prototype and set up web analytics to track which features are most popular. Once it launches, we'll announce the site on our social media feeds and buy search and display ads to acquire visitors. Our goal is to receive 50 new visitors per day to the site from the month of June and see a 10 percent increase in store sales.

Since we're not as focused on customer loyalty, we won't plan on building an app, e-mail database, or mobile loyalty program right away, but these tactics will go on our longer-term roadmap.

It's important to note that measuring sales across channels has proved to be difficult. At first, marketers were under the impression that *the last click wins*, or the idea that the last place a customer was before they made a sale, is the one who deserves credit for the sale. That means, if a customer sees a mobile display ad for a product, later searches for it, researches it on a website, but then buys after seeing a deal on social media, the sale would be attributed to social media. Today, marketers are working on developing multitouch attribution models that span a customer's path to purchase across devices and tactics.

Although there is debate about the number of times a consumer must receive a brand message before he or she actually makes a purchase,* one study demonstrated that 10 times is optimal before the consumer starts to get annoyed.[1] This reinforces the need for omni-channel marketing in order to integrate the many ways that brands push messages out to consumers through a variety of media in order to help them make a purchase decision.

Another Marketer's Thoughts on Mobile

After speaking to Jeffrey Donnell, Product Development & Innovation Manager at Whirlpool Corporation, we wanted to share some of his thinking and insights.

---

* http://en.wikipedia.org/wiki/Effective_frequency

Jeff had an interesting perspective on brands leveraging mobile and he coined them *pocket brands*. When we asked why, he explained,

> Since we constantly monitor our lives via our mobile devices we have a very high connection to the devices themselves as we truly rely on them. Combine that with the fact that they aren't limited by space, location, or connectivity, making the number of interactions potentially endless. Then, you have a high *sticky* factor, the ideal place for brands. Put that in your pocket and you have "pocket branding."

In terms of being a successful *pocket brand*, Jeff offered,

> In order to be successful, it's not simply about exposure anymore. Now you have to create a benefit in consumers' minds using their internal value equation. Mobile is constantly asking for inputs from the user, so now the only way to guarantee sustainable use from the end user is to make sure the output is greater than that input. That's a lot tougher to do in practice, because you have to literally predict what consumers are going to view as valuable, especially considering the pace at which those things change.

Jeff's message highlights the importance of understanding the people you market to and building a smart mobile strategy to meet their needs and cater to their wants. Ultimately, a strong foundation will help your brand become a memorable *pocket brand*.

Exercise to Learn Concepts

Examine the mobile tactics used by a mass transit brand (i.e., Amtrak, Southwest Airlines, Chicago Transit Authority (CTA), and others). If this brand had used the N.O.T.E. framework:

1. Which consumer needs do the mobile tactics answer?
2. Which business objectives do the tactics work to accomplish?
3. Which metrics are they probably using to measure success?

4. How does this campaign use push and/or pull tactics?

5. What recommendations do you have for the brand moving forward?

Exercise to Apply Concepts

Apply the N.O.T.E. framework to your favorite brand to create a mobile strategy.

Additional Resources

Mobile marketing is constantly evolving. To stay current or get more information, look to the following resources.

Industry Websites and Best Practices

Mobile Marketing Association Best Practices: http://www.mmaglobal.com/education/bestpractice

Mobile Marketing Association Case Study Hub: http://www.mmaglobal.com/case-study-hub/

Google Webmasters Guide to Building Smartphone-Optimized Websites: https://developers.google.com/webmasters/smartphone-sites/

Email Best Practices from Mail Chimp: http://mailchimp.com/resources/research/email-on-mobile-devices/html/#section-best-practices-for-mobile-email

Email Design Formats Explained from Litmus: https://litmus.com/blog/defining-and-understanding-mobile-email-approaches

Mobile Advertising Creative Guidelines from the IAB and MMA: http://www.iab.net/guidelines/508676/508767/mobileguidelines

Mobile Rising Stars Ad Units: http://www.iab.net/risingstarsmobile#1

Industry News, Events, and Job Listings

Mobile Marketer / Mobile Commerce Daily: http://mobilemarketer.com/

MediaPost's Mobile Marketing Daily: http://www.mediapost.com/publications/mobile-marketing-daily/

TechCrunch: http://techcrunch.com/mobile/

Mashable: http://mashable.com/mobile/

Mobile Monday Meetups: http://www.mobilemonday.net

Key Terms

All terms are customized for the mobile age by Molly Garris.

CHAPTER 1

mobile marketing: marketing on or with a mobile device, such as a smartphone.[1]

smartphone: a mobile phone with more advanced computing capability and connectivity than basic feature phones.[2] While both can typically browse the web, smartphones also have the ability to access and download apps for a richer mobile experience, amongst other features.

operating system (OS): An operating system (OS) is a software that manages computer hardware resources and provides common services for computer programs. The operating system is an essential component of the system software in a computer system. Application programs usually require an operating system to function. Operating systems can be found on almost any device that contains a computer—from cellular phones and video game consoles to supercomputers and web servers.* On mobile, the most popular operating systems are Android and iOS.

feature phone: lower-cost cell phones that may have the ability to talk, text, and browse but do not have access to proprietary app stores like iOS App Store or Google Play.

mobile data infrastructure: A digital infrastructure promoting data sharing and consumption.†

data snacking: to consume small snippets of information when time permits.‡

---

* http://en.wikipedia.org/wiki/Operating_system
† http://en.wikipedia.org/wiki/Data_infrastructure
‡ http://www.netlingo.com/word/data-snacking.php#sthash.sU7a7hD6.dpuf

mobile advertisements: a form of advertising, typically search or display, via mobile (wireless) phones or other mobile devices. It is a subset of mobile marketing.*

CHAPTER 2

copper line: telephone line or telephone circuit (or just line or circuit within the industry) is a single-user circuit on a telephone communication system. Typically, this refers to the physical wire or other signaling medium connecting the user's telephone apparatus to the telecommunications network, and usually also implies a single telephone number for billing purposes reserved for that user.

interactive voice response (IVR) systems: a technology that allows a computer to interact with humans through the use of voice and dual-tone multi-frequency signaling (DTMF) tones input via keypad.†

video teleconferencing: the conduct of a videoconference (also known as a video conference or video teleconference) by a set of telecommunication technologies that allow two or more locations to communicate by simultaneous two-way video and audio transmissions. It has also been called *visual collaboration* and is a type of groupware.‡

native phone functionality: features embedded or born on a mobile phone, such as texting, calling, or taking a photo.§

short messaging system, or SMS: text messaging service component of mobile device or tablet. It uses standardized communications protocols to allow fixed line or mobile phone devices to exchange short text messages using 160 characters or less.[3]

call-to-action: is an instruction to the audience to provoke an immediate response, usually using an imperative verb such as *call now to find out more* or *visit a store today*.¶

---

* http://en.wikipedia.org/wiki/Mobile_advertisings

† http://en.wikipedia.org/wiki/Interactive_voice_response

‡ http://en.wikipedia.org/wiki/Video_conferencing

§ Garris (2014).

¶ http://homebusiness.about.com/od/homebusinessglossar1/g/Call-To-Action-Definition.htm

opt-in: Of a selection, the property of having to choose explicitly to join or permit something; a decision having the default option being exclusion or avoidance; used particularly with regard to mailing lists and advertisements.*

open rates: a measure primarily used by marketers as an indication of how many people *view* or *open* the commercial e-mail they send out. It is most commonly expressed as a percentage and calculated by dividing the number of e-mail messages opened by the total number of e-mail messages sent (excluding those that bounced).[4]

geo-fenced text alerts: A geo-fence is a dynamically generated location—as in a radius around a store or other location. When an opted-in mobile device enters this radius, or geo-fence, a text message notification may be sent. This notification might contain information about a local deal, a nearby location or other location-sensitive information.[5]

premium text messaging: Premium messaging is an option to purchase or subscribe to messaging programs, provided by third-party content providers, for premium charges (e.g., charges that are in addition to standard messaging charges). The premium charges may be one-time charity donations or recurring subscriptions for content like ringtones. These programs are initiated through specially provisioned short codes.

multimedia messaging service or MMS: is a standardized way to send messages that include multimedia content, like photos, and videos, to and from mobile phones. It is a one-size-fits-all approach.[†]

rich media messaging, or RMM: is a customized way to send messages that include multimedia content, like long text, photos and video. RMM is a patented messaging technology that delivers device-optimized rich content to virtually any handset on the market using Intelligent Handset Detection (IHD).[‡]

push versus pull campaign: a push campaign drives people to a marketing initiative, like direct mail or e-mail. Whereas, a pull campaign

---

* http://en.wiktionary.org/wiki/opt-in
† http://en.wikipedia.org/wiki/Multimedia_Messaging_Service
‡ http://www.irismobile.com/?page_id=83

is one that enables people to find a marketing initiative, like search or a website.*

instant messaging (IM) apps: is a type of online chat, which offers real-time text transmission over the Internet. Some IM applications can use push technology to provide real-time text, which transmits messages character by character, as they are composed. More advanced instant messaging can add file transfer, clickable hyperlinks, Voice over IP, or video chat.†

mCRM: Customer relationship management, or CRM, is a system for managing a company's interactions with current and future customers. It involves using technology to organize, automate, and synchronize sales, and for marketing, customer service, and technical support.[6] mCRM or mobile CRM is the use of mobile technology for managing customer relationships via activities like SMS, MMS, RMM, e-mail and push notifications.‡

click-through rates: is a way of measuring the success of an online advertising campaign for a particular website as well as the effectiveness of an e-mail campaign by the number of users who clicked on a specific link.[7]

transaction rates: another way of measuring the success of an online advertising campaign for a particular website as well as the effectiveness of an e-mail campaign by the number of users that took a particular predefined action, that is, clicked to call, clicked to map, bought a product, etc.§

churn: In its broadest sense, it is a measure of the number of individuals or items moving out of a collective group over a specific period of time. It is one of two primary factors that determine the steady-state level of customers a business will support. The term is used in many contexts, but is most widely applied in business with respect to a contractual customer base.¶

open rate: is a measure primarily used by marketers as an indication of how many people *view* or *open* the commercial electronic mail, or e-mail, they send out. It is most commonly expressed as a percentage and

---

* Modified by Garris (2014).
† Modified by http://en.wikipedia.org/wiki/Instant_messaging
‡ Garris and Mishra (2014).
§ Garris (2014).
¶ http://en.wikipedia.org/wiki/Churn_rate

calculated by dividing the number of e-mail messages opened by the total number of e-mail messages sent (excluding those that bounced.)[8]

channel knowledge: education and experience using a marketing channel, such as text messaging*

opt-out: An action available to unsubscribe or exit; used particularly with regard to mailing lists and advertisements[†]

CHAPTER 3

mobile search: is an evolving branch of information retrieval services that is centered on the convergence of mobile platforms and mobile phones, or that it can be used to tell information about something and other mobile devices.[‡]

clicks: a single click selects (or highlights) an object while double-clicking executes or opens the object. Touchscreen mobile phones only offer a single-touch experience but the industry measures in these touches using the word clicks.[§]

click to call: is a form of mobile web-based communication in which a person clicks an object (e.g., button, image, or text) to request an immediate connection with another person in real-time by a phone call.[¶]

omni-channel experience: is the evolution of multichannel retailing, but is concentrated more on a seamless approach to the consumer experience through all available shopping channels, that is, mobile internet devices, computers, brick-and-mortar storefronts, television, radio, direct mail, catalog, and so on. To use all channels simultaneously, and retailers using an omni-channel approach will track customers across all channels, not just one or two. In the brick-and-mortar channel, digitally savvy consumers are entering stores already well-informed about a

---

* Garris (2014).

† Garris (2014).

‡ http://en.wikipedia.org/wiki/Mobile_search

§ http://en.wikipedia.org/wiki/Point_and_click#Single_click

¶ http://en.wikipedia.org/wiki/Click-to-call

product's features and prices, and expect store employees to know more than they do.[9]

optimized: Mobile optimization is the process of modifying a website's design template and code base to be easily viewed on a mobile device.[*]

Flash animation: is an animated film, common to interactive websites, which is created by Adobe Flash or similar animation software. The term Flash animation not only refers to the file format but to a certain kind of movement and visual style.[†]

HTML5 code: is a core technology markup language of the Internet used for structuring and presenting content for the World Wide Web. It is the fifth revision of the HTML standard (created in 1990 and standardized as HTML 4 as of 1997) and, as of December 2012, is a candidate recommendation of the World Wide Web Consortium (W3C). Its core aims have been to improve the language with support for the latest multimedia while keeping it easily readable by humans and consistently understood by computers and devices (web browsers, parsers, etc.).[‡]

responsive design: is a web design approach aimed at crafting sites to provide an optimal viewing experience—easy reading and navigation with a minimum of resizing, panning, and scrolling—across a wide range of devices (from mobile phones to desktop computer monitors).[10]

replatform: completely rebuild a mobile website[§]

---

[*] Garris (2014).

[†] http://en.wikipedia.org/wiki/Flash_animation

[‡] "HTML5 Differences from HTML4" (April 2011), Introduction:"HTML 4 became a W3C Recommendation in 1997. While it continues to serve as a rough guide to many of the core features of HTML, it does not provide enough information to build implementations that interoperate with each other and, more importantly, with a critical mass of deployed content. The same goes for XHTML1, which defines an XML serialization for HTML4, and DOM Level 2 HTML, which defines JavaScript APIs for both HTML and XHTML. HTML5 will replace these documents."

[§] Garris (2014).

stacking navigation: A website that offers a vertical list, or stack, of clickable links to direct a user to more content. This navigation is common on mobile, since horizontal space is limited.*

cost per click (CPC): is an internet advertising model used to direct traffic to websites, in which advertisers pay the publisher (typically a website owner) when the ad is clicked. It is defined simply as "the amount spent to get an advertisement clicked."[11]

cost per mille (CPM): also called cost % and cost per thousand (CPT) (in Latin *mille* means thousand), is a commonly used measurement in advertising. It is used in marketing as a benchmarking metric to calculate the relative cost of an advertising campaign or an ad message in a given medium.[12]

usability: is the ease of use and learnability of a human-made object. In this instance, the object of use is a website and how it performs on mobile.†

CHAPTER 4

mobile app: is a downloadable piece of software designed to run on smartphones, tablet computers, and other mobile devices (e.g., iPod Touch). The term *app* is a shortening of the term *application software*. It has become very popular and in 2010 was listed as "Word of the Year" by the American Dialect Society.‡

features and functionalities: The way something works or operates, or online, what purpose it serves.§

pre-installed: refers to software, typically apps, that are already installed and licensed on a computer or smartphone when the device is purchased.[13]

---

* Garris (2014).

† http://en.wikipedia.org/wiki/Usability

‡ 'App' voted 2010 word of the year by the American Dialect Society (UPDATED) American Dialect Society". Americandialect.org. on January 8, 2012. Retrieved January 28, 2012.

§ See more at: http://www.netlingo.com/search.php#sthash.t3gqJ2o1.dpuf

download apps: means to receive data to a local system from a remote system, or to initiate such a data transfer.*

branded apps: mobile apps published by a brand marketer (e.g., Skittles, Marriott Hotels or Lexus)

paid apps: mobile apps that require payment prior to or during the initial install

free-mium: is a pricing strategy by which a product or service (typically a digital offering such as software, media, games, or web services) is provided free of charge, but money (premium) is charged for proprietary features, functionality, or virtual goods.[14]

virtual good: is a nonphysical object or currency purchased for use in online communities or online games. Virtual goods have no intrinsic value and are intangible by definition.[15]

media buy: A sub function of advertising management, it is the procurement of media real estate at an optimal placement and price.†

organic downloads: occur when an app is downloaded based on a person's search results, or based on the person discovering the app on the top charts or curated placement within an app store.‡

push notifications: describes a style of Internet-based communication where the request for a given transaction is initiated by the publisher or central server. App push notifications can be turned on or off by the user and can be used as a form of mCRM to drive users back into an app.§

code base: is used in software development to mean the whole collection of source code used to build a particular application or component.¶

hybrid app: run on the device, and are written with web technologies (HTML5, CSS, and JavaScript). Hybrid apps run inside a native container,

---

* http://searchnetworking.techtarget.com/definition/downloading

† http://en.wikipedia.org/wiki/Media_buying

‡ Garris (2014).

§ http://en.wikipedia.org/wiki/Push_notifications

¶ http://en.wikipedia.org/wiki/Code_base

and leverage the device's browser engine (but not the browser) to render the HTML and process the JavaScript locally. A web-to-native abstraction layer enables access to device capabilities that are not accessible in mobile web applications, such as the accelerometer, camera, and local storage.[*]

churn: in its broadest sense, it is a measure of the number of individuals or items moving out of a collective group over a specific period of time.[†] In this instance, app churn is number of times an app was deleted in a period of time divided by the total number of app installations in the same period. The less the churn, the better; it signifies a retained customer base.

tutorials: is a method of transferring knowledge and may be used as a part of a learning process.[‡] Many app and game developers require new users to complete a brief tutorial prior to its first use. This helps eliminate confusion and can aid in retention.

frequency of use: is the number of occurrences of a repeating event per unit time.[§] In this context, frequency of use refers to how often mobile users return to open and use an installed app.[¶]

CHAPTER 5

optimize for mobile: The process of modifying a website's design template and code base to be easily viewed on a mobile device.[**]

social platforms: The name of the platform that runs social networking services.[††]

Fans and Follows: Fans and Followers are consumers who "like" your brand on social media.[‡‡] Networks use different names for these

---

[*] http://en.wikipedia.org/wiki/Hybrid_application

[†] http://en.wikipedia.org/wiki/Churn_rate

[‡] http://en.wikipedia.org/wiki/Tutorial

[§] http://en.wikipedia.org/wiki/Frequency

[¶] Garris and Mishra (2014)

[**] Garris (2014).

[††] http://www.netlingo.com/word/social-platform.php#sthash.BlyboZwb.dpuf

[‡‡] http://www.hadeninteractive.com/likes-fans-follows-understanding-social-media-terminology/

consumers, for example, Facebook calls them Fans and Twitter calls them Followers.

super fans: who show a great deal of enthusiasm for something, such as a sports team or entertainer.* This is a commonly used term for active and engaged brand fans on social media.

social CRM: Customer relationship management, or CRM, is a system for managing a company's interactions with current and future customers. It involves using technology to organize, automate, and synchronize sales, and for marketing, customer service, and technical support.[16] Social CRM is the use of social technology for managing customer relationships via activities like Facebook posts, Tweets, and other social communications with the brand.†

visual storytelling: or a visual narrative, is a story told primarily through the use of visual media. The story may be told using still photography, illustration, or video, and can be enhanced with graphics, music, voice, and other audio.

earned impressions: when information about your brand is voiced by your customer, in the absence of any compensation or value exchanged.‡

CHAPTER 6

context: is the situation in which something happens, or the group of conditions that exist where and when something happens.§

content: is information and experiences that provides value for an end-user or audience in specific contexts.[17]

mobile display: is a general name for a mobile ad that typically contains text (i.e., copy), logos, photographs, or other images to communicate a product or service.¶

---

* http://en.wikipedia.org/wiki/Superfan
† Garris (2014).
‡ Garris (2014).
§ http://www.merriam-webster.com/dictionary/context
¶ http://en.wikipedia.org/wiki/Display_advertising

standardization: the process of creating uniformity, or templates, to drive efficiencies*

standard mobile banner (or standard display ad): consists of placing a predefined size of a graphical banner, static or interactive, on a mobile website or mobile app.[†]

adhesion banner: is a type of mobile banner ad that remains adhered to the bottom of a browsing experience, constantly remaining above the fold and in the line of sight.[‡]

interstitial ad: is a type of mobile banner ad that appears in the browsing experience and requires a user to take action (click a box, advance a photo gallery, etc.) before continuing their experience.[§] Interstitial ads are a form of interruption marketing.[18]

rich media ad: A type of mobile banner that offers highly engaging mobile experiences through advanced interactions that leverage the phone's features and functionalities.[¶]

expandable banner: An expandable ad is a rich media ad that changes dimensions upon a predefined condition, such as the user's click on the ad, or the user turning their phone from portrait to landscape. Expanding ads allow advertisers to fit more information into a restricted ad space.[19]

mCommerce: The act of buying a good or service via mobile device.[**]

site or app skin: A branded background, static or interactive, designed to integrate seamlessly into an existing mobile experience.[††]

native ad: A proprietary publisher ad format that integrates into a mobile experience in a more natural, editorial, and streamlined way.[‡‡]

---

* Garris (2014).

[†] http://en.wikipedia.org/wiki/Website_monetization

[‡] Garris (2014).

[§] Garris (2014).

[¶] Garris, 2014.

[**] Garris (2014).

[††] Garris (2014).

[‡‡] Garris (2014).

social mobile ad: An ad served on a social media network that encourages brand engagement and participation.*

preroll ad: A video ad served before an online video stream.

video ad: advertisements that play video, often in short form and within other streaming sites or apps. Some advertisers re-purpose their TV ads, or simply *cut them down* to be a shorter version than their TV counterparts. Better practices are emerging to ensure quality, engaging creative.[20]

mobile sponsorship: occurs when a brand negotiates media placement as a single, dominant advertiser within an existing mobile site or app.†

location-based advertising: occurs when a person shares their phone's location and in turn, an advertisement is targeted based on this location‡

retargeting: A data mining technique in which marketers assemble computerized databases of customer information to create profiles of users who will be most receptive to their messages. § Many desktop websites will begin serving ads to you after you've visited their website. Knowing that you've already taken an interest in a product, they hope to convert you from a browser to a buyer.

frequency capping: technology that limits the number of times your display ads appear to the same person

cookies: a small file that a web server automatically sends to your PC when you browse certain websites. Cookies are stored as text files on your hard drive so servers can access them when you return to websites you've visited before.¶

first-party cookies: data gathered by advertisers through a direct relationship with a web visitor. It could include registration data, purchase history, or other data points to target or cater ads to them.**

---

* Garris (2014).
† Garris (2014).
‡ Garris (2014).
§ http://www.netlingo.com/dictionary/t.php
¶ http://www.netlingo.com/dictionary/c.php
** http://blog.isocket.com/2013/09/the-difference-between-first-and-third-party
-data/

programmatic buying: The term covers a wide range of technologies that have begun automating the buying, placement, and optimization of advertising, replacing human-based methods like phone calls, faxes, and in-person meetings. Through programmatic technologies, advertisers can buy ads the way they pick up something on Amazon or bid on eBay.

programmatic simply means automated: A lot of people confuse it with buying ads through computer-run auctions (known as real-time bidding) but that's just one way to buy ads programmatically. At its core, programmatic buying is any ad buy that gets processed through machines.*

real-time bidding (RTB): refers to the means by which ad inventory is bought and sold on a per-impression basis, via programmatic instantaneous auction, similar to financial markets.†

return on investment (ROI): is the concept of an investment of some resource yielding a benefit to the investor.‡

multiple touch points: describes the interface of a product, service, or brand with customers or users, noncustomers, employees and other stakeholders, before, during, and after a transaction. This may be applied in business-to-business as well as business-to-consumer environments.§

integrated strategy: is defined by David Aaker as a process that can allow an organization to concentrate its resources on the optimal opportunities with the goals of increasing sales and achieving a sustainable competitive advantage. Marketing strategy includes all basic and long-term activities in the field of marketing that deal with the analysis of the strategic initial situation of a company and the formulation, evaluation, and selection of market-oriented strategies and therefore contribute to the goals of the company and its marketing objectives.[21] An integrated strategy is one in which all of the 4Ps work together at the outset to maximize consumer communication.[22]

emotion: A short-term feeling that drives behavior.[23]

---

* http://www.netlingo.com/dictionary/p.php

† http://en.wikipedia.org/wiki/Real-time_bidding

‡ http://en.wikipedia.org/wiki/Return_on_investment

§ http://en.wikipedia.org/wiki/Touchpoint

static: A term used to denote that something is not dynamic, meaning that it remains the same. In the case of mobile advertising, it's a creative image that does not move and cannot be clicked.*

animated banner ad: A display unit with movement to attract a user's attention. It can be clickable or not.

interactive banner ad: A display unit that allows a person to click or engage with it, typically switching content when engaged.

dynamic banner ad: display unit with a predetermined creative structure but changeable text or imagery based on an input. For example, an auto manufacturer might invite people to test drive and based on their location, a dynamic banner could populate the name of the nearest auto dealership.

CHAPTER 7

branded content: content published by a brand, including images, video, articles, social media posts, infographics, and more.

pull tactics: marketing tactics made available for consumers looking to *pull* information to make a purchase decision. These tactics can include earned properties like websites, mobile apps, and presence on social media.

push tactics: marketing tactics strategically messaged, or *pushed*, to consumers to trigger brand re-engagement. These tactics can include e-mail, SMS/MMS/RMM, app push notifications and more.

quick-response codes (QR codes): A two dimensional image that, once scanned by a QR code reader app, can be decoded to generate an action on the person's device. For example, the code can trigger a phone number to populate for easy dialing, a website to load, or even a text message to populate. The codes are often used as a short cut to additional content or engagement, and this format of 2D code is becoming a standard form of content delivery around the globe.

---

* http://www.netlingo.com/word/static.php#sthash.SAUaTDpg.dpu

Texting (or text messaging): is the act of composing and sending a brief, electronic message between two or more mobile phones.*

call to action: is an instruction to the audience to provoke an immediate response, usually using an imperative verb such as "call now to find out more" or "visit a store today."†

keyword: is a unique, preconfigured word that triggers a response from the short code of a mobile messaging campaign. For example, if an auto manufacturer offers buyers to opt in for warranty information and other relevant news, they might use a call to action like, text ALERTS to 12345 for monthly news updates. However, if the local dealership wants to offer exclusive service offers and news, they might also communicate a call to action like, text CHIWESTLOOP for deals from our accessories and service department. Both keywords, ALERTS and CHIWESTLOOP would be configured to reply with a double opt-in message but once subscribed, message content is determined by the opt-in keyword.

shortcode: are special, shortened telephone numbers, used to support SMS, MMS, and RMM campaigns. In the United States, short codes can have four, five or six digits and it's used to connect a person to a machine, which helps automate requests to opt-in and opt-out. Shortcodes can be leased from the Common Short Code Association (CSCA) and need to be provisioned by a mobile aggregator prior to running a campaign.

near field communication (NFC): allows communication or simple transactions between two devices, triggered by touching them together or bringing them into very close proximity, usually no more than a few centimeters away.‡ NFC chips contain information and can be read by any device capable of detecting it. Some marketers are embedding NFC chips into print or in-store shelf ads, allowing NFC-enabled phones to engage with a brand's content.

---

* http://en.wikipedia.org/wiki/Texting

† http://homebusiness.about.com/od/homebusinessglossar1/g/Call-To-Action
-Definition.htm

‡ http://connectstrong.com/resources/what-is-a-nfc-chip/

image recognition (or object recognition): technology embedded into a mobile app that leverages the phone's camera to find and identify objects, people, places, buildings, and more

image matching: A functionality that analyzes visual content and identifies matching images between a query image and a reference database*

audio recognition: technology imbedded into a mobile app that leverages a smartphone's microphone to capture sound and identify the source of that sound, that is, a song, a TV show, a TV ad, or a movie

augmented reality technology (AR): ability to overlay data on to what a smartphone sees in the real world when using an AR-powered app. The phone's compass, GPS, and accelerometer help to continuously feed the app data to present the most relevant content available.

location-based services (LBS): general class of computer program-level services that use location data to control features.[24]

CHAPTER 8

N.O.T.E. framework: strategic mobile marketing framework developed by Molly Garris in 2014.

website analytics: The measurement, collection, analysis, and reporting of web data for purposes of understanding and optimizing web usage. Popular web analytics tools include Google Analytics, Web Trends, Adobe SiteCatalyst, to name a few.

search engine marketing: a form of Internet marketing that involves the promotion of websites by increasing their visibility in search engine results pages (SERPs) through optimization and advertising.[25]

---

* http://www.ltutech.com/technology/image-matching/

Advance Quotes for
A Beginner's Guide to
Mobile Marketing

The authors have the brilliant ability to take something quite complicated and distill it into understandable simplicity. Every marketer should read this to ensure they "get" this rapidly emerging space.

—Chris Bridgland, Director, Digital Strategy
at Leo Burnett Chicago

The authors provide a case study driven view of mobile strategies, how they work, and expected results. It is refreshing to see a holistic view on mobile that focuses on strategy and results instead of leading decisions based on technology. This book is a must read for every marketer!

—Cezar Kolodziej, President, CEO and
co-founder of Iris Mobile

The concept of "pocket branding" is excellent and this book has established its first pocket brand for mobile marketing texts.

—Dr. J. Steven Kelly, DePaul University,
Associate Professor of Marketing

This is a must read for any digital marketer.

—Roy Wollen, President, HANSA Marketing and
Adjunct Professor at DePaul University

This is a great way to confirm what you thought you knew and learn quickly what you didn't know in a mobile snacking manner!

—April Carlisle, SVP Global Shopper Marketing
at Arc Worldwide

This "clearly captures the hurdles marketers face as trying to convince their brands to make big bets in emerging media."

—Elizabeth Elliott, Associate Director at
Starcom MediaVest Group

The digital world moves lightning fast and has many facets. The information provided is easily digestible and provides a solid understanding of mobile search for entry level search staff or those at the executive level looking for a functional understanding of mobile search.

—Chris Kenallakes, Kenshoo

The world of marketing changed when we all started carrying our computers in our pockets. Garris and Mishra do a great job clearly outlining the challenges and the opportunities that presents us as marketers.

—Jim Tobin, President, Ignite Social Media
Author of Social Media is a Cocktail Party
and Earn It. Don't Buy It.

In mobile, everything is changing in every year, but what we should know is what is not easily changing, consumers' insights of mobile. This book allows beginners to easily understand status quo and practical application of mobile marketing, but the real value of this book is it does not miss what's the real value of mobile marketing – "insight."

—Professor Chang Dae Ham, Assistant Professor
of Advertising, The University of Illinois

The book gives clear examples of the different marketing strategies that other companies have employed in their campaigns and presents well explained case studies that give the reader insights into the possibilities of mobile marketing.

—Joy Liuzzo, Principal, Product Marketing
(Connected Devices) at Amazon

Notes

Introduction

1. Schultz, Tannenbaum, and Lauterborn (1993).

Chapter 1

1. Hinkle (2014).
2. MarketingCharts Staff (2014).
3. Dolcourt (2013).
4. comScore (2014).
5. Dolcourt (2013).
6. "Overall Wireless Network Problem Rates Differ Considerably Based on Type of Service" (2013).
7. Bernoff (2013).
8. Zickuhr and Rainie (2014).
9. Mobile Behavior Report (2014).
10. Harvard Business Review Magazine (2013).
11. Walsh (2012).
12. "Digital Set to Surpass TV in Time Spent with US Media" (2013).
13. Forrester (2013).
14. *eMarketer* (2013).
15. Mobile Behavior Report (2014).
16. comScore (2013).
17. Ask (2013).

Chapter 2

1. Associated Press (2013).
2. Sterling (2014).
3. Mallow, Taylor, and Reilly (2013).
4. Oliverez-Giles (2013).
5. Kluger. (2012).
6. Pew Research Internet Project (2014).
7. French (2014).
8. "2014 State of Marketing" (2014).

9. Dusto (2013).
10. Pepitone (2010).
11. "Mobile Messaging Trends" (2013).
12. Hazlett (2013).
13. "Mobile Messaging Trends" (2013).
14. Cashmere Agency (2013).
15. Stampler (2013).
16. H. Smith (2014).
17. "Mobile Messaging Trends" (2013).
18. Jitender (2012).
19. Pilon (2014).
20. "Mobile Marketing Economic Impact Study" (2013).
21. "Designing for the Mobile Inbox" (2014).
22. Experian Marketing Services (2013).

Chapter 3

1. Quinn (2013).
2. The Nielsen Company (2013).
3. Google/Ipsos MediaCT/Purchased (2014).
4. Kilcourse (2011).
5. Kilcourse (2011).
6. Schultz, Tannenbaum, and Lauterborn (1993).
7. Rangaswamy, and Van Bruggen (2005).
8. Husson (2013).
9. Lee (2014).

Chapter 4

1. "comScore MobiLens Three-Month Average ending in December 2013" (2013).
2. Perez (2013).
3. Brustein (2013).
4. Kumparak (2014).
5. Sawyers (2012).
6. Khalaf (2013).
7. Graham (2013).
8. Greenberg (2013).
9. Perez (2013).

10. Osborne (2013).
11. Paramis (2013).

Chapter 5

1. Fox (2013).
2. Aquino (2013).
3. Murphy (2011).
4. Neilsen (2009).
5. Lacy (2013).
6. Doyle (2013).
7. Knowledge@Wharton (2014).

Chapter 6

1. Yu (2013).
2. Park and Salvendy (2012).
3. Fulgoni and Lipsman (2014).
4. Constine (2014).
5. Essany (2013).
6. "MMA and IAB Release 'Mobile Phone Creative Guidelines' For Public Comment" (2013).
7. eMarketer (2012).
8. Rosenkrans and Myers (2012).
9. Lacy (2014).
10. Yu (2013).
11. C. Smith (2014).
12. Sikka (2014).
13. O'Mahony (2013).
14. Albergotti (2014
15. Heine (2013).
16. L. Johnson (2013).
17. theScore (2014)
18. Boyle (2014)
19. Bager (2013).
20. Yu (2013).
21. Hoelzel (2014).
22. Rosenkrans and Myers (2012).
23. PointRoll (2013)

24. Fulgoni and Lipsman (2014).
25. Fulgoni and Lipsman (2014, 14).
26. Arc Worldwide (2013).
27. Park and Salvendy (2012).
28. Park and Salvendy (2012).
29. Park and Salvendy (2012).

Chapter 7

1. IHS Pressroom (2014).
2. Tode (2012).
3. Scoble and Isreal (2014).
4. D. Johnson (2013).
5. O'Neill (2012).

Chapter 8

1. Pride and Ferrell (2014).

Key Terms

1. Karjaluoto and Leppäniemi (2005).
2. Nusca (2009).
3. Kelly (2012).
4. Arnold (2011).
5. de Lara and LaMarca (2008).
6. Shaw (1991).
7. *American Marketing Association Dictionary* (2012). The Marketing Accountability Standards Board (MASB) endorses this definition as part of its ongoing Common Language: Marketing Activities and Metrics Project.
8. John Arnold (April 2011).
9. Multimedia Plus Research (n.d).
10. Gillenwater (2010).
11. Farris et al. (2010). The Marketing Accountability Standards Board (MASB) endorses the definitions, purposes, and constructs of classes of measures that appear in *Marketing Metrics* as part of its ongoing Common Language: Marketing Activities and Metrics Project.
12. *American Marketing Association Dictionary* (2012). The Marketing Accountability Standards Board (MASB) endorses this definition as part of its ongoing Common Language: Marketing Activities and Metrics Project.

13. Microsoft (2014).
14. de la Iglesia and Gayo (2008).
15. Wauters (2007)
16. Shaw (1991).
17. Odden (2013).
18. Hanley and Becker (2007).
19. Interactive Advertising Bureau (2012).
20. Broadband TV News (2010).
21. Aaker (2008).
22. Lauterborn (1990).
23. Park and Salvendy (2012).
24. Quercia et al. (2010).
25. Search Engine Land (2007).

References

Albergotti, R. 2014. "Facebook Answers Critics with Mobile-Ad Surge." *The Wall Street Journal*, July 23. http://online.wsj.com/articles/facebook-results-keep -surging-on-mobile-ad-growth-1406146246

Aquino, C. 2013. "Putting the Digital Future in Focus: Key Trends that Will Shape the U.S. Digital Industry in 2013." comScore. http://www.comscore .com/Insights/Blog/Putting-the-2013-U.S.-Digital-Future-in-Focus (accessed November 19, 2014).

Arc Worldwide. 2013. "Beautiful Hair Whatever the Weather." Brand Activation Association. http://www.baalink.org/reggie-case-study/beautiful-hair-whatever -weather

Ask, J.A. 2013. "Getting Mobile Right with Mobility POST." Forrester. https://www.forrester.com/Getting+Mobile+Right+With+Mobility+POST/ fulltext/-/E-RES94541

Associated Press. 2013. "Big Disconnect: Phone Companies Abandoning Copper Phone Lines." *Tampa Bay Times*. http://www.tampabay.com/news/business/ big-disconnect-phone-companies-abandoning-copper-phone-lines/2130508

Bager, A. 2013. "Mobile Cookies Don't Necessarily Crumble." *ClickZ*, November 19. http://www.clickz.com/clickz/column/2307773/mobile-cookies-don-t -necessarily-crumble

Bernoff, J. 2013. "Introducing the Mobile Mindshare Index." Forrester Research. http://blogs.forrester.com/josh_bernoff/13-04-25-introducing_the_mobile _mind_shift_index_may_1_webinar

Boyle, C. 2014. "Top Trends in Mobile Location-Based Advertising." eMarketer, March 20. http://www.slideshare.net/eMarketerInc/emarketer-webinar-top -trends-in-mobile-locationbased-advertising

Brustein, J. 2013. "The Profitable Future of Free Mobile Apps." *Bloomberg Business Week*. http://www.businessweek.com/articles/2013-09-19/the -profitable-future-of-free-mobile-apps

Cashmere Agency. 2013. "Kik Messenger: Aquafina X the Art of the Chase Sticker Pack." http://cashmereagency.com/tag/kik-messenger/

comScore. 2013. "The Six Most Used Social Networks on Mobile in the U.S." Mashable, December. http://mashable.com/2014/04/03/social-media-mobile- chart/

"comScore MobiLens Three-Month Average ending in December 2013." 2013. comScore. https://www.comscore.com/Products/Audience_Analytics/ MobiLens (accessed November 8, 2014).

comScore. 2014. "comScore Reports April 2014 U.S. Smartphone Subscriber Market Share." https://www.comscore.com/Insights/Press_Releases/2014/6/comScore_Reports_April_2014_US_Smartphone_Subscriber_Market _Share

Constine, J. 2014. "The Most Important Insights from Mary Meeker's 2014 Internet Trends Report." *TechCrunch*, May 28. http://techcrunch.com/gallery/mary-meeker-internet-trends/slide/9/

Dolcourt, J. 2013. "Smartphone Innovation: Where We're Going Next (Smartphones Unlocked)." *cnet*. http://www.cnet.com/8301-17918_1 -57578982-85/smartphone-innovation-where-were-going-next -smartphones-unlocked/

Doyle, M. 2013. "Social Media Stats of 2013." The Website Marketing Group, September 5. http://blog.twmg.com.au/social-media-stats-of-2013-infographic/

Dusto, A. 2013. "An ACE Hardware Store Nails Its First Mobile Marketing Campaign." Internet Retailer. http://www.internetretailer.com/2013/09/05/ace-hardware-store-nails-its-first-mobile-marketing-campaign

eMarketer. 2013. "Mobile Fact Pact: A Guide to Mobile Marketing," July. http://adage.com/trend-reports/report.php?id=81

eMarketer. 2012. "U.S. Digital Ad Spending Trends For 2012." http://www.emarketer.com/newsroom/index.php/emarketer-webinar-key-digital -trends-2012/

"Digital Set to Surpass TV in Time Spent with US Media." 2013. eMarketer, August 1. http://www.emarketer.com/Article/Digital-Set-Surpass-TV-Time -Spent-with-US-Media/1010096

"Mobile Messaging Trends." 2013. eMarketer. http://www.emarketer.com /Webinar/Mobile-Messaging-TrendsTapping-SMS-Mobile-Email -Push/4000069

Essany, M. 2013. "Emarketer: Mobile Ad Spending to Climb 95% This Year." Mobile Marketing Watch, August 21. http://www.mobilemarketingwatch .com/emarketer-mobile-ad-spending-to-climb-95-this-year-35424/

"Mobile Behavior Report." 2014. ExactTarget. http://www.exacttarget.com/sites/exacttarget/files/deliverables/etmc-2014mobilebehaviorreport.pdf

"Designing for the Mobile Inbox." 2014. ExactTarget. http://image.exct.net/lib/fe641570776d02757515/m/2/EN-DesigningForMobileInbox.pdf

"2014 State of Marketing." 2014. ExactTarget. http://content.exacttarget.com/en/StateOfMarketing2014?ls=Blog&lss=Blog.StateofMarketing2014& lssm=Corporate&camp=701A0000000g9GuIAI

Experian Marketing Services. 2013. "Experian Marketing Services 2013 Q2 Email Benchmark Study." http://www.experian.com/marketing-services/email-marketing-quarterly-benchmark-study-q2-2013.html?WT.srch=PR _EMS_Q213Benchmark_082813_press

Forrester. 2013. "How US Consumers Shop on Mobile Devices." Performics, May. http://www.performics.com/assets/1/7/Industry_Updates_on_Key _Mobile_Trends_5_17_13.pdf

Fox, Z. 2013. "65% of Time Spent on Social Networks Happens on Mobile." *Mashable*, October 25. http://mashable.com/2013/10/24/content -consumption-desktop-mobile/?utm_cid=mash-com-g+-pete-photo

French, S. 2014. "SMS Is Best: Your Mobile Priorities Might Be Overrated, Underperforming." *Wired*. http://www.wired.com/2014/03/sms-best -mobile-priorities-might-overrated-underperforming/

Fulgoni, G., and A. Lipsman. 2014. "Digital Game Changers: How Social Media Will Help Usher in the Era of Mobile and Multi-Platform Campgin-Effectiveness Measurement." *Journal of Advertising Research*, pp. 11–16.

Google/Ipsos MediaCT/Purchased. May 2014. "Understanding Consumers' Local Search Behavior." http://think.storage.googleapis.com/docs/how -advertisers-can-extend-their-relevance-with-search_research-studies.pdf

Graham, J. 2013. "Instagram Before Eggs? Which App Starts Your Morning?" *USA Today*, November 2. http://www.usatoday.com/story/tech/columnist/ talkingtech/2013/11/02/app-morning-instagram/3290631/

Greenberg, K. 2013. "Forrester on in-App Ads: Do It Right or Go Home." *MediaPost News*, September 30. http://www.mediapost.com/publications/ article/210229/forrester-on-in-app-ads-do-it-right-or-go-home .html?edition=65229#ixzz2gTlhpmZd

Harvard Business Review Magazine. 2013. "Vision Statement: How People Really Use Mobile." http://hbr.org/2013/01/how-people-really-use-mobile

Hazlett, A. 2013. "Express Opts for Rich Media Messaging to Boost Sales." Mashable. http://mashable.com/2013/12/16/express-holiday-metrics/

Heine, C. 2013. "75% of Mobile Video Ads Happen in-App Study Also Finds That Shorter, Non-Skippable Spots Excel." *Adweek*, April 24. http:// www.adweek.com/news/technology/75-mobile-video-ads-happen -app-157217

Hinkle, A. 2014. "Marketing to the On-Demand Consumer." Media Post: Email Insider. http://www.mediapost.com/publications/article/206856/marketing -to-the-on-demand-consumer.html#axzz2eVhXETGZ

Hoelzel, M. 2014. "THE PROGRAMMATIC ADVERTISING REPORT: Mobile, Video, and Real-Time Bidding Will Catapult Programmatic Ad Spend." *Business Insider*, July 15. http://www.businessinsider.com/the -programmatic-ad-report-2014-7

Husson, T. 2013. "Understanding the Gap between Consumers' and Marketers' Use of Mobile." *Forrester*, August 1. https://www.forrester.com/ Understanding+The+Gap+Between+Consumers+And+Marketers +Use+Of+Mobile/fulltext/-/E-RES98561

IHS Pressroom. 2014. "NFC-Enabled Cellphone Shipments to Soar Fourfold in Next Five Years." http://press.ihs.com/press-release/design-supply-chain/nfc -enabled-cellphone-shipments-soar-fourfold-next-five-years

"MMA and IAB Release 'Mobile Phone Creative Guidelines' for Public Comment." 2013. *Interactive Advertising Bureau*, January 25. http://www.iab .net/about_the_iab/recent_press_releases/press_release_archive/press _release/pr-012513_mobile

"Overall Wireless Network Problem Rates Differ Considerably Based on Type of Service." 2013. *J.D. Power*. http://www.jdpower.com/content/press-release/ sP8rA2r/2013-u-s-wireless-network-quality-performance-study-volume-2.htm

Jitender, M. 2012. "78% of US Email Users Will Also Access Their Email via Mobile by 2017." Forrester Research. http://blogs.forrester.com/jitender _miglani/12-10-18-78_of_us_email_users_will_also_access_their_emails _via_mobile_by_2017

Johnson, D. 2013. "SMS Open Rates Exceed 99%." *SMS Marketing* (Blog), http://www.tatango.com/blog/sms-open-rates-exceed-99/

Johnson, L. 2013. "Unilever's Axe Targets Tech-Savvy Males via App Sponsorship." Mobile Marketer, June 10. http://www.mobilemarketer.com/cms/news /content/15516.html

Khalaf, S. 2013. "Flurry Five-Year Report: It's an App World. The web just lives in it." Flurry. http://blog.flurry.com/bid/95723/Flurry-Five-Year-Report-It-s -an-App-World-The-Web-Just-Lives-in-It

Kilcourse, B. 2011. "Gaming Google: The Growing Importance of Omni-Channel." Retail Systems Research. http://www.rsrresearch.com/2011/03/01/ gaming-google-the-growing-importance-of-omni-channel/

Kluger, J. 2012. "We Never Talk Any More: The Problem with Text Messaging." *CNN*. http://www.cnn.com/2012/08/31/tech/mobile/problem-text -messaging-oms/index.html

Knowledge@Wharton. 2014. "The Ignored Side of Social Media: Customer Service." Forbes, January 2. http://www.forbes.com/sites/ knowledgewharton/2014/01/09/22014/

Kumparak, G. 2014. "Flappy Bird Is Gone from the App Store." TechCrunch. http://techcrunch.com/2014/02/09/flappy-bird-remove-from-app-store/

Lacy, L. 2013. "Burts Bees Vines Cast Products in Classic Lit in #6second Classics." *ClickZ*, October 14. http://www.clickz.com/clickz/news/2300257/ burt-s-bees-vines-cast-products-in-classic-lit-in-6secondclassics

Lacy, L. 2014. "Toyota Speaks to Consumers with Voice Activated Mobile Ads." *ClickZ*, January 14. http://www.clickz.com/clickz/news/2322385/toyota -speaks-to-consumers-with-voice-activated-mobile-ads

Lee., J. 2014. Google Testing In-Store Conversions Tied to AdWords Ads." *Search Engine Watch*, April 15. Retrieved from http://searchenginewatch.com

/article/2340074/Google-Testing-In-Store-Conversions-Tied-to-AdWords-Ads

Mallow, M.L., J.D. Taylor, and C. Reilly. 2013. "The New Written Consent Requirements for Telemarketing Calls Under the TCPA Go into Effect on October 16, 2013 - are you ready?" Lexology. http://www.lexology.com/library/detail.aspx?g=f7402bd7-65d0-4cd4-9dc8-38421e2bcabc

MarketingCharts staff. 2014. "7 in 10 US Mobile Subscribers Now Own a Smartphone." MarketingCharts, June 4. http://www.marketingcharts.com/wp/online/7-in-10-us-mobile-subscribers-now-own-a-smartphone-43114/attachment/comscore-smartphone-share-of-mobile-subscriber-market-oct2011-apr2014-june2014/

"Mobile Marketing Economic Impact Study." 2013. *Mobile Marketing Association.* http://www.mmaglobal.com/whitepaper/mobile-economic-impact-study

Murphy, D. 2011. "Social Mobile on the Increase in the US." *Mobile Marketing Magazine*, October 20. http://www.mobilemarketingmagazine.com/content/social-mobile#foQu2fqVxwjjL8P4.99

Neilsen. 2009. "Global Advertising Consumers Trust Real Friends and Virtual Strangers the Most." Neilsen Global Online Consumer Survey. http://www.nielsen.com/us/en/newswire/2009/global-advertising-consumers-trust-real-friends-and-virtual-strangers-the-most.html

O'Mahony, J. 2013. "Mark Zuckerberg Fails to Console Facebook Shareholders by Admitting 'Disappointment'." *The Telegraph*, June 12. http://www.telegraph.co.uk/technology/facebook/10115357/Mark-Zuckerberg-fails-to-console-Facebook-shareholders-by-admitting-disappointment.html

O'Neill, C. 2012. "How Push Notifications Can Boost Your Mobile Strategy." Econsultancy, August 24. https://econsultancy.com/blog/10596-how-push-notifications-can-boost-your-mobile-strategy-3

Oliverez-Giles, N. 2013. "Smartphone Video Calling Has Tripled Since 2011, Says Pew Center." The Verge. http://www.theverge.com/2013/9/19/4750232/pew-center-21-percent-of-americans-make-video-calls

Osborne, C. 2013. "Malicious Apps, Mobile Malware Reaches 1 Million Mark." ZDNet, October 1. http://www.zdnet.com/malicious-apps-mobile-malware-reaches-1-million-mark-7000021371/

Paramis, J. 2013. "Are You a Rarity? Only 16% of People Will Try Out an App More than Twice." Digital Trends, March 12. http://www.digitaltrends.com/mobile/16-percent-of-mobile-userstry-out-a-buggy-app-more-than-twice/

Park, T., and G. Salvendy. 2012. "Emotional Factors in Advertising via Mobile Phones." *International Journal of Human-Computer Interaction* 28, no. 9, pp. 597–612.

Pepitone, J. 2010. "Text Donations Raise $7M for Red Cross Haiti Effort." *CNN*. http://money.cnn.com/2010/01/14/technology/haiti_text_donation/

Perez, S. 2013. "Users Have Low Tolerance for Buggy Apps—Only 16% Will Try a Failing App More than Twice." TechCrunch. http://techcrunch.com/2013/03/12/users-have-low-tolerance-for-buggy-apps-only-16-will-try-a-failing-app-more-than-twice/

Pew Research Internet Project. 2014. "Mobile Technology Fact Sheet." http://www.pewinternet.org/fact-sheets/mobile-technology-fact-sheet/

Pilon, A. 2014. "Mobile Email Survey: Privacy and Security Moderately Concerning." AYTM. https://aytm.com/blog/daily-survey-results/mobile-email-survey-2/

PointRoll. 2013. "2013 Benchmarks." http://demo.pointroll.net/content/demos/marketing/2013benchmarks/2013_PointRoll_Benchmarks_Final.pdf

Pride, W.M., and O.C. Ferrell. 2014. *Marketing.* Cengage Learning.

Quinn, C. 2013. "5 Things SMBs Can Do to Optimize for Mobile Search." *Street Fight*, September 10. http://streetfightmag.com/2013/09/10/5-things-smbs-can-do-to-optimize-for-mobile-search/

Rangaswamy, A., and G.H. Van Bruggen. Spring 2005. "Opportunities and Challenges in Multichannel Marketing: An Introduction to the Special Issue." *Journal of Interactive Marketing* 19, no. 2, pp. 5–11.

Rosenkrans, G., and K. Myers. 2012. "Mobile Advertising Effectiveness." *International Journal of Mobile Marketing* 7, no. 3, pp. 5–24.

Sawyers, P. 2012. "Neilsen: US Smartphones Have an Average of 41 Apps Installed, Up from 32 Last Year. *The Next Web.* http://thenextweb.com/insider/2012/05/16/nielsen-us-smartphones-have-an-average-of-41-apps-installed-up-from-32-last-year/

Schultz, D.E., S.I. Tannenbaum, and R.F. Lauterborn. 1993. *Integrated Marketing Communications: Putting It Together & Making It Work.* New York: McGraw-Hill. http://www.amazon.com/Integrated-Marketing-Communications-Putting-Together/dp/0844233633/ref=sr_1_1?ie=UTF8&qid=1383847122&sr=8-1&keywords=lauterborn

Scoble, R., and S. Isreal. 2014. *The Age of Context.* Patrick Brewster Press.

Sikka, P. 2014. "Mobile Becoming the Main Driver of Twitter's Revenue Growth." *Yahoo! Finance*, May 1. http://finance.yahoo.com/news/mobile-becoming-main-driver-twitter-130019958.html

Smith, C. 2014. "Native Ads Will Be the Centerpiece of All Social Media Advertising in the Near Future." *Business Insider*, November 27. http://www.businessinsider.com/native-mobile-ads-dominate-social-media-2013-11

Smith, H. 2014. "Get Schooled by Taco Bell." Down the Wire. http://blog.telegraphbranding.com/tag/2014/

Stampler, L. 2013. "Taco Bell Just Snapchatted a Bunch of Customers." *Business Insider.* http://www.businessinsider.com/taco-bell-sends-burrito-snapchat-to-fans-2013-5

Sterling, G. 2014. "Mobile-Centric Households Now Outnumber those with Landlines in US." *Internet 2GO.* http://internet2go.net/news/data-and -forecasts/mobile-centric-households-now-outnumber-landlines-us

The Nielsen Company. 2013. *Mobile Search Moments: Understanding How Mobile Drives Conversions.* ssl.gstatic.com/think/docs/creating-moments-that -matter_research-studies.pdf

theScore. 2014. "Thescore Hits Home Run with Jack Link's." Press Release. http:// mobile.thescore.com/2013/08/thescore-hits-home-run-with-jack-links/

Tode, C. 2012. "Kraft NFC Pilot Delivers 12 Times the Engagement Level of QR Codes." *Mobile Commerce Daily,* October 18. http:// www.mobilecommercedaily.com/kraft-nfc-pilot-delivers-12-times-the -engagement-level-of-qr-codes

Walsh, M. 2012. "Smartphones Don't Outperform Feature Phone Preferences." *Online Media Daily.* http://www.mediapost.com/publications/ article/168895/?print#axzz2f0UbZ5uo

Yu, J.H. 2013. "You've Got Mobile ads! Young Consumers' Responses to Mobile Ads with Different Types of Interactivity." *International Journal of Mobile Marketing* 8, no. 1, pp. 5–22.

Zickuhr, K., and L. Rainie. 2014. "Tablet and E-reader Ownership." *Pew Research Internet Project.* http://www.pewinternet.org/2014/01/16/tablet-and-e -reader-ownership/

Key References

Aaker, D. 2008. *Strategic Market Management*. Hoboken, NJ: John Wiley & Sons. ISBN 978-0-470-05623-3

American Dialect Society. January 8, 2011. "'App' Voted 2010 Word of the Year by the American Dialect Society (UPDATED)." *Americandialect.org*. http://www.americandialect.org/app-voted-2010-word-of-the-year-by-the-american-dialect-society-updated (accessed January 28, 2012).

American Marketing Association Dictionary 2012. https://www.ama.org/resources/Pages/Dictionary.aspx?dLetter=C#click-through+rate+%28ctr%29 (accessed November 2, 2012).

Arnold, J. April 2011. "Calculating the Open Rate for Your E-Mail Marketing Campaign." In *E-Mail Marketing For Dummies*. 2nd ed. Hoboken, NJ: Wiley Publishing, Inc.

Broadband TV News. 2010. *84.1% of US Internet Users View Web Video*, November 15. http://www.broadbandtvnews.com/2010/11/15/84-1-of-us -internet-audience-viewed-online-video/

de la Iglesia, J.L.M., and J.E.L. Gayo. 2008. "Doing Business by Selling Free Services." In *Web 2.0: The Business Model*.1–14. New York: Springer

De Lara, E., and A. LaMarca. 2008. "Synthesis Lectures on Mobile and Pervasive Computing." *Location Systems: An Introduction to the Technology behind Location Awareness*. ed. M. Satyanarayanan, 88. San Rafael, CA: Morgan & Claypool Publishers. ISBN 978-1-59829-581-8.

Farris, P.W., N.T. Bendle, P.E. Pfeifer, and D.J. Reibstein. 2010. *Marketing Metrics: The Definitive Guide to Measuring Marketing Performance*. Upper Saddle River, NJ: Pearson Education, Inc. ISBN 0-13-705829-2.

Gillenwater, Z.M. December 15, 2010. "Examples of Flexible Layouts with CSS3 Media Queries." In *Stunning CSS3*, 320. Berkeley, CA: New Riders. ISBN 978-0-321-722133.

Hanley, M., and M. Becker. 2007. "Cell Phone Usage and Advertising Acceptance among College Students: A Four-Year Analysis." *2008 AEJMC Conference: Advertising Division–Research*. Chicago, IL. http://citation.allacademic.com/meta/p_mla_apa_research_citation/2/7/2/3/4/pages272340/p272340-3 .php (accessed June 13, 2013).

"HTML5 Differences from HTML4". 2011. Working Draft World Wide Web Consortium, April 5.

Interactive Advertising Bureau. (September 27, 2012) April 16, 2013. *Mobile Rich Media Ad Interface Definitions (MRAID) v. 2.0.* http://www.iab.net/media/file/IAB_MRAID_v2_FINAL.pdf (accessed June 13, 2013).

Karjaluoto, H., and M. Leppäniemi. 2005. "Factors Influencing Consumers' Willingness to Accept Mobile Advertising: A Conceptual Model." International Journal of Mobile Communications 3, no. 3, pp. 197–213.

Kelly, H. 2012. "The Text Message Turns 20." *CNN,* December 3. http://edition.cnn.com/2012/12/03/tech/mobile/sms-text-message-20/

Lauterborn, B. 1990. "New Marketing Litany: Four Ps Passé: C-Words Take Over." *Advertising Age* 61, no. 41, pp. 26–27.

Microsoft. 2014. *Pre-installed on a New Computer.* http://windows.microsoft.com/en-gb/windows-8/meet

Multimedia Plus Research. 2014. "How to Improve the Customer Experience with App-Based, On-Floor Associate Training." http://www.multimediaplus.com/improve-experience-with-app-based-training/

Nusca, A. 2009. "Smartphone vs. Feature Phone Arms Race Heats Up; Which Did You Buy?" *ZDNet,* August 20. http://www.zdnet.com/blog/gadgetreviews/smartphone-vs-feature-phone-arms-race-heats-up-which-did-you-buy/6836 (accessed December 12, 2011).

Odden, L. 2013. "What is Content? Learn from 40+ Definitions." *TopRank Online Marketing Blog.* http://www.toprankblog.com/2013/03/what-is-content/ (accessed February 20, 2014).

Park, T., and G. Salvendy. 2012. "Emotional Factors in Advertising via Mobile Phones." *International Journal of Human-Computer Interaction* 28, pp. 597–612.

Quercia, D., N. Lathia, F. Calabrese, G. Di Lorenzo, and J. Crowcroft. 2010. "Recommending Social Events from Mobile Phone Location Data." *2010 IEEE International Conference on Data Mining.* 971–976. Sydney, Australia: IEEE. doi:10.1109/ICDM.2010.152. ISBN 978-1-4244-9131-5.

Search Engine Land. 2007. "The State of Search Engine Marketing 2006," February 8. http://searchengineland.com/the-state-of-search-engine-marketing-2006-10474 (accessed June 7, 2007).

Shaw, R. 1991. *Computer Aided Marketing and Selling.* Newton, MA: Butterworth Heinemann. ISBN 978-0-7506-1707-9

Wauters, R. 2007. "Virtual Goods: The Next Big Business Model." *techcrunch.com,* June 20. http://techcrunch.com/2007/06/20/virtual-goods-the-next-big-business-model/

Index

CPSIA information can be obtained at www.ICGtesting.com
Printed in the USA
LVOW01s2251060815

449113LV00020BA/1116/P